Michael Boyce was born in Stapleton, a suburb of Bristo'⁣ ⁣ ⁣ ⁣ ⁣ ⁣ ⁣ ⁣ ⁣ ⁣ ⁣ ⁣ and
his wife now live in a village in South Gloucestersh⁣⁣⁣ ⁣ ⁣ ⁣ ⁣ ⁣ ⁣ ⁣ ⁣ ⁣ ⁣ ⁣ d
daughter having long since left the family b⁣⁣

As a structural engineer, he wo⁣⁣'
latterly a construction company, and
reports and a number of technical paper⁣ ⁣ ⁣ ⁣ ⁣ ⁣ ⁣ ⁣ ⁣ ⁣ ⁣ ⁣ ⁣ ⁣ ⁣ ⁣ al
engineering consultancy practice, eventu⁣

Like many men of his age, he lived ⁣⁣ ⁣ ⁣ ⁣ ⁣ ⁣ ⁣ ugh the Second
World War, and now enjoys reading abou⁣ ⁣ ⁣ ⁣ ⁣ ⁣ ⁣ ⁣s of warfare and the
exploits of those who fought in various c ⁣⁣⁣icts. He remembers seeing
ambulance convoys passing his home, carrying wounded to the American
hospital at Frenchay, a few miles north of Bristol. Still living within a
'stone's throw' of the now NHS Frenchay Hospital, he read about its history,
including the period when the Americans cared for their wounded, in a book
written by a doctor who worked in the hospital after the war.

Having always enjoyed writing, he believes that his wartime recollections,
together with the Frenchay hospital history, provided the incentive to research
the American hospital at Tyntesfield and its use after the war, and this book is
the fruits of that research.

TYNTESFIELD

★ ★ ★ IN WWII

MICHAEL BOYCE

Published in 2012 by the author using SilverWood Books Empowered Publishing®
SilverWood Books
30 Queen Charlotte Street, Bristol BS1 4HJ
www.silverwoodbooks.co.uk

ISBN 978-1-78132-071-6

British Library Cataloguing in Publication Data
A CIP catalogue record for this book is available from the British Library

Set in Bembo by SilverWood Books
Printed on paper sourced responsibly

TYNTESFIELD IN WWII

Contents

Acknowledgements

The greater part of this book deals with two United States Army hospital units that operated at Tyntesfield, England in World War Two: the 56th and 74th General Hospitals. The records of these units are to be found only in US repositories. The hospitals' personnel were US citizens and most of their patients were US servicemen and women, and survivors mostly now live in the United States. So, when I started my research for this book, I knew that the major source of material would be in the United States. I also knew that, without the convenience of the Internet and emails, I would never have started.

Sixty-odd years after the war ended, despite appeals placed on a number of WWII-related websites, tracing people who served with the 56th and 74th General Hospitals or were their patients proved to be virtually fruitless. So, instead, I decided to contact 'official' sources. Initially, the first two were *The US National Archives and Records Administration (NARA)*, and the historical branch of the *US Army Medical Department (AMEDD)*. Both yielded much valuable information. And, as my research continued, I acquired useful contacts in the States. A number of these suggested other possible sources of information and other avenues to pursue.

Therefore, without the help of many people, this book could never have been written. This statement has, perhaps, become a tired old favourite to include in the acknowledgements section of a book. Nonetheless, it is unquestionably true. Some individuals, websites and books contributed little other than to confirm known facts; others contributed hugely, and, of these, I would particularly like to thank the following and note, where appropriate, their specific contributions:

In America

Dr Sanders Marble, a senior historian with AMEDD untiringly gave his time in guiding me through the workings of a typical US military hospital in WWII. He provided me with copies of official *Signal Corps* photographs taken at Tyntesfield and directed me elsewhere when he could not answer some of my questions.

Winston Hawkins, a Staff Sergeant with the 56th General Hospital and organiser of the unit's annual reunions, sent me copies of more than thirty photographs relating to the 56th during its time in Europe. He also provided me with a number of stories about his time with the unit.

At the end of March 2011, I received an email from a lady named Molly Sheehan Placko. She told me that her father was the commanding officer of the 56th General Hospital, and that she had many photographs and other information from her late father's time in England, France and Belgium. Molly had earlier been in contact with Jim Scott whose father, Capt Robert Scott, served as a surgeon with the 56th. Jim scanned Molly's photographs and sent them on to me, as well as providing me with copies of some of his father's photographs, and many are included in this book.

Alice Boehret, a nurse with the 74th General Hospital donated all of her letters home, these having been saved by family and friends, to the Special Collections Library of the University of Tennessee, Knoxville. Alice's letters provide an exceptional insight into life as a nurse in a UK military hospital in WWII. Cynthia Tinker of the Center for the Study of War and Society at the University of Tennessee kindly sent me copies of all of Alice's letters together with photographs of the 74th GH at Tyntesfield. I have quoted extensively from Alice's letters and thank Cynthia for this privilege.

The Betty H Carter Women Veterans Historical Project University of North Carolina at Greensboro also holds a collection of memorabilia donated by Alice Boehret, together with a transcript of an oral interview conducted with her in May 2000. For copies of items in the collection and permission to quote from the interview, I am indebted to Beth Ann Koelsch, curator of the project at Greensboro. Also, Beth Ann put me in touch with Alice's niece, Celeste Boehret Price, who has enthusiastically given me much additional personal information about Alice, unavailable elsewhere.

The US Library-of-Congress Veterans History Project, Washington DC, sent me a copy of *Benjamin Dangerfield 3rd's War Experiences*. Ben served with the 56th General Hospital in England and Europe. After reading his diary, I was fortunate in being able to correspond with him by email, and he happily gave permission for me to quote from his *War Experiences*, and added some additional memories about his time with the 56th.

In the United Kingdom

Fran and Martin Collins, an English couple, authors of a number of books about US hospitals elsewhere in England, gave me a copy of an early 56th GH report and other helpful information about US hospitals in the UK in WWII.

Barrie Porter prepared the layout drawings of the hospital buildings based on an original drawing in the 56th GH archives, an RAF aerial photograph, and a drawing by Long Ashton Rural District Council prepared in connection with final demolition of the hospital buildings. He also prepared the typical ward layout based upon an original drawing in the 56th GH archives and a survey by the author of an almost identical surviving ward at Fremmington, Devon.

Somerset Records Office allowed me to examine and quote from the minutes of Long Ashton Rural District Council relating to Tyntesfield and its adjacent villages.

John Penny, a Bristol historian, provided me with details about Luftwaffe operations over Bristol and the West Country. And he helped me immensely with general guidance and in extracting still photographs from videos and films.

David Knights, Bill Cunningham, Freda Vowles and Doris Christie (via sister Phyllis Horman and Peter Wright) provided their recollections of living in the Tyntesfield 'village'.

And, finally, other individuals and organisations in America and the UK who assisted me in more minor yet valuable ways.

Tyntesfield National Trust; the staff of Yate Public Library, South Gloucestershire; WW2 US Medical Research Centre; Ken Reeves, curator of Kington Museum for the photograph of Kington Camp water tower; Tony Honeyman; Warren Hower; Philip C Grinton, Lt Col US Army (retired) provided me with lists of US military units stationed at Tyntesfield; Steve Jebson, a library information officer with the British Met Office at Exeter, provided me with detailed weather information for relevant times; David Hogg for Gibbs family information; Ray Llewellyn for much knowledge about Tyntesfield and local people; Ed Souder, Tracey Brake, John Thiessen, Martin Weeks and Joe Wring.

Author's Notes

Some official records have been found to be incomplete and factual contradictions occur within them. Moreover, contradictions arise between official records and other sources of information, including the recollections of local people. Where appropriate, I have endeavoured to present a balanced version of conflicting information. I have corrected obvious errors – village and town names misspelt, and occasionally misplaced in the UK.

I have made all reasonable efforts to obtain permission to directly quote from published material, but locating authors and publishers of works sixty years old has sometimes been impossible. Nonetheless, I have quoted directly from some material without permission, have acknowledged the source, and trust that, if the authors read this book, they will accept my apologies and understand my difficulty. Many contemporary photographs have done the rounds in the United States and, in most instances, their origins are unknown. Therefore, I have acknowledged the source from which I obtained copies.

In a book of this kind, the use of some technical words is unavoidable. Providing definitions for every unfamiliar or technical word is clearly not possible, so I hope that the reader will have some idea of their meanings, or derive their meanings from the context in which they are used. However, some words and terms are unlikely to be in the reader's vocabulary, 'guano' for example, and some words are mainly of American origin like 'musette bag'. Where such words and terms are used, I have provided a brief definition enclosed in square brackets, thus [...].

Strictly speaking, *America* and *the United States* are not the same – *America* refers to the continent and *United States* to the states within the continent. But today, people commonly call a person from the United States an American. Therefore, I have used both terms interchangeably when referring to the country and to its people.

All photographs in the book are of Tyntesfield except as identified otherwise. Photographs were taken using an assortment of cameras by people with varying skills, so qualities vary. Moreover, they were all scanned at various levels of resolution from original prints, also influencing their quality. Purists may argue that historic photographs should be reproduced without being reworked in any way. However, I have chosen to modify all by reproducing them as black-and-white images. I have adjusted the contrast and brightness of some, and I have cropped some to a size to suit the book layout. By transforming photographs, I hope I have not offended any readers.

Introduction

The Second World War brought hardship and a way of life that most British people had never before experienced. The war brought shortages of food, fuel and other simple luxuries that peacetime normally provided. And people living in North Somerset towns and villages like Clevedon, Nailsea, Failand and Wraxall did not escape the hardship. For them, the war brought the night-time blackout, wailing air-raid sirens and the drone of German bombers flying overhead on their way to bomb the city of Bristol, the aircraft factory at Filton, and Portishead and Avonmouth docks. At night, people of North Somerset would stand in their gardens or in the streets and stare at the crimson sky over Bristol, less than five miles to the north-east, as fires ravaged its buildings. And, occasionally, they would experience the terror of aircraft crashing nearby, or bombs cratering their farmland, inaccurately dropped or jettisoned by the over-flying bombers on their way to or returning from their targets. But the people in these North Somerset towns and villages carried on with the austere, unvarying normality of their changed lives; that is, until the summer of 1943 when war brought to their villages a new phenomenon: the American soldier – the Yank.

The Americans brought with them some of the luxury items that most local people had not seen since the war started. They brought oranges and tinned fruit, chocolate and chewing gum, and real coffee. They brought other things that many people had never seen before: peanut butter, American cigarettes, Coca-Cola, nylon stockings, left-hand drive lorries and Jeeps, baseball, the black man, swing music and the jitterbug dance. And they brought a contradictory blend of brashness and charm unfamiliar to the more reserved British people.

But the Americans were not here on holiday; they were here to prepare for war. American servicemen and women came to the United Kingdom to be part of the mighty force that would invade France in June 1944, and ultimately bring about the defeat of Nazi Germany and end the war. Many had arrived in Bristol in mid-summer 1942 to run the huge war-materials storage depots in Bristol, and to unload American ships at Bristol and Avonmouth docks. But it was not until about a year later that the big build-up of Americans in the West Country truly got underway. By the start of 1944, many training camps had sprung up in the countryside and villages neighbouring Bristol, with more than twenty in North Somerset alone.

And war created its inevitable horrors in the form of bodies mutilated in training and on the battlefield, so the Americans needed many hospitals in which to care for their casualties. The Tyntesfield Estate proved to be an ideal location on which to operate one such hospital. So, late in 1942, builders moved onto a piece of quiet pastureland to convert it into a little piece of America. From November 1943 to May 1944, the 56th General Hospital cared for its wounded and sick soldiers from the training camps; and, from May 1944 to June 1945, the 56th having moved on, the 74th General Hospital cared for its battle casualties from the fighting in mainland Europe. And, on another part of the Tyntesfield estate, American engineers built a tented 'transit' camp where as many as 1,500 soldiers stopped off for a few days or weeks on their way to fight in the war on mainland Europe.

But, by the autumn of 1944, most of the nearby American camps had been abandoned, soldiers having moved on to join the fight on mainland Europe. And, by the end of June 1945, the hospital had also been abandoned, the 74th having left Tyntesfield to set up a hospital in France. So, the familiar sight of American soldiers in their smart uniforms walking around the villages, drinking in the pubs, and handing out gum and nylon stockings was no more. Their departure left a hole in the lives of many local people.

After the Americans left, the local authority, urgently in need of accommodation for many homeless civilians and soldiers returning from fighting in the war, converted many of the redundant hospital buildings into self-contained dwellings, thereby creating the 'Tyntesfield Village'. But this village too was abandoned by 1960, the buildings demolished and the land returned to its former use.

This book tells the story of the two American Army hospital units that operated at Tyntesfield, and of their work in Europe after leaving England. It recounts the experiences of some of the Americans who worked in the hospital, and of some of the many local ladies who also helped out there. And it tells of the village and its residents who lived in the converted hospital buildings after the Americans had gone.

Chapter One

The Tyntesfield Estate

Tyntesfield: *a Spectacular Victorian Gothic Revival house with gardens and parkland*. Thus, its present owner, the British National Trust, describes Tyntesfield. The estate, in the Parish of Wraxall, Somerset, lies approximately seven miles south-west of Bristol by road, a few miles from Nailsea and about seven miles from Clevedon. Since it purchased the house and part of the original estate in 2002, the National Trust has progressively refurbished the house and its gardens, and it now attracts about 200,000 visitors every year.

The estate came into being in the early years of the fifteenth century when the Tynte family, local medieval landowners, acquired the land, though details of the acquisition are unclear. Over the following four centuries or so, ownership passed on through the family until 1813 when John Penrose Seymour, owner of the adjoining Belmont Estate, purchased it for his son the Reverend George Turner Seymour. An appealing feature of the estate was that it lay on a gently sloping hillside. Making good use of the feature, in 1820 the Reverend built a Gothic villa and gardens on a terraced plateau partway up the hillside that provided superb views of the surrounding countryside to the south-west. In 1843, Reverend Seymour died and his widow sold the estate in April 1844 to William Gibbs for £21,295-3s.

William, the second son of Antony Gibbs had, by the early years of the nineteenth century, become a successful businessman. He traded with Spain, exporting British textiles and importing Spanish merino wool, fruit and wine. Following the disruption to Spanish trade during the Napoleonic Wars, the Gibbs' family business, with William now a partner, looked elsewhere to trade, and began to build a lucrative business in South America. Beginning in 1842, the family firm imported guano [dried seabird droppings] from Peru and, from 1861, nitrates from Bolivia and Chile. Nineteenth century farmers used both products extensively as fertilisers in Britain and Europe.

By the early 1860s, the company having flourished, William Gibbs decided to develop the house into a property more befitting his wealth and status in society. So, between 1862 and 1864, by progressive additions and alterations to the house, he transformed it into a substantial mansion, roughly doubling the size of the original villa. During this period also, he enhanced the grounds by extensive remodelling and planting rare trees and conifers. Some years later, he acquired the neighbouring estates of Belmont to the east, and Charlton to the north-west. In 1873, Gibbs commissioned designs for a private chapel to be added to the house, but sadly he died in 1875 just before the work was completed. His wife Matilda, however, ensured that work continued and the chapel was fittingly completed.

In 1887, the estate passed to William and Matilda Gibbs' son Antony, who embarked upon further improvements to the house through 1887-90. Colonel George Abraham Gibbs, son of Antony, succeeded him in 1907, the previous year having been elected Member of Parliament for Bristol West. In 1921, Colonel Gibbs was appointed Treasurer to the Royal Household. On his retirement from office, in the New Year's Honours of 1928, he was created a baron, thereby becoming the first Baron Wraxall of Clyst St George. He died in 1931, leaving his widow Lady Ursula Mary to bring up two young sons and manage the estate, which she did most successfully. When she died in 1979 at the age of ninety-one, the estate passed on to the elder son, George Richard Lawley Gibbs, who became the second Lord Wraxall.

George never married and, in his later years, led a relatively solitary life, living in only a few rooms of the mansion. From his mother's death in 1979 to his own passing in 2001, George's somewhat reclusive living style allowed the building and its contents to deteriorate. Following his death, none of the family wanted to take on responsibility for or to live in the property so, in 2002, the estate's trustees sold the house and much of its grounds to the British National Trust. Soon after buying the property, the National Trust embarked upon a programme of work to restore the house and its gardens to their grander days.

World War II

The Second World War visited Tyntesfield in diverse ways.

Tyntesfield experienced war first-hand during a daylight raid on the Bristol Aeroplane Company works at Filton on Wednesday 25 September 1940. On that day, five high-explosive bombs and one oil bomb fell onto open land of the estate and the garden of Home Farm. The explosions badly damaged two cottages and farm outbuildings, shattered the farmhouse windows, and fractured a water main, cutting the supply to Tyntesfield House. Subsequently, an unexploded bomb was discovered fifty yards from another cottage.

During another raid, in the dark, early morning hours of Wednesday 5 June 1941, this time centred on the Portishead and Avonmouth docks, eighteen small high-explosive bombs fell across the Tyntesfield estate. Starting at Charlton Lodge on the Clevedon/Failand to Bristol road, they fell in a line down the estate road from Upper Lodge to Tyntesfield Farm and

Tyntesfield House – View from north-west. Note diagonal paper strips on windows to limit shattering from bomb blast. (University of Tennessee)

continued across the estate, one falling very close to the Tyntesfield House chapel. The explosions shattered windows, damaged ceilings, brought down telephone lines, killed three cows and seriously injured four others.

Bristol, with its docks, industrial areas and neighbouring aircraft production works, and its rail links to other major British cities, featured high on the Luftwaffe's target list. The city experienced its first air raid on the night of 19 June 1940 when bombers released their deadly cargoes mostly in the Portishead area, a long way from their intended targets of Filton aircraft works and Avonmouth docks. The Luftwaffe carried out further sporadic raids over the next five months, culminating in the first major raid on Sunday 24 November 1940. The main targets for the 135 bombers which droned over the city were the docks and surrounding industrial buildings. High-explosive and incendiary bombs destroyed some dockside buildings and tragically gutted much of the historic central area of the city, including its main shopping centre. Bombs also fell on roads and properties in the city's suburbs, including the smart residential area of Clifton.

Clifton High School for Girls, located in the Clifton suburb, provided a high-class education, with boarders figuring among its pupils. Following the major November raid on Bristol, the school head Miss Glenday, recognizing the potential danger to the girls and her responsibility to their parents, decided to evacuate about thirty of the senior girl boarders out of schooling time to a safer area. So, with Lady Wraxall's consent, Miss Glenday arranged overnight and weekend accommodation for herself and the girls in rooms of Tyntesfield House from January 1941 to the war's end. For daytime lessons, a bus shuttled the girls to school at Clifton and returned them to Tyntesfield late afternoon.

Two soldiers sitting on grass bank outside Tyntesfield house main entrance. (University of Tennessee)

But perhaps the greatest changes the war brought to the routine of life at Tyntesfield and its neighbouring villages came with the construction of many camps to house soldiers of the American army; notable among them being a hospital on the estate. From late 1943 to the middle of 1945, approximately 650 American servicemen and women lived in and operated the hospital; and, at the start of 1945, more than 1,200 casualties would lie in its ward beds.

After the war

By the end of June 1945, the Americans had gone. For a while British military units used the hospital buildings for various purposes and then responsibility eventually transferred to Long Ashton Rural District Council. But what was it to do with the camp and its empty buildings? Fortunately, a solution readily presented itself. Faced with a chronic housing shortage, the council converted many of the hospital buildings into dwellings as a part-solution to its housing problem. Families whose homes had been demolished by the bombing, returning servicemen and women who had nowhere to live, and other displaced persons took up residence in the homes. But, by the end of 1959, all had been rehoused on estates built in nearby towns. A demolition company moved on to the 'village' and soon all the buildings had disappeared and the land returned to the estate. Today, almost nothing remains to show that it ever existed.

Chapter Two

America Enters the War

At 6:00am on Sunday 7 December 1941, Lieutenant Mitsuo Matsuzaki, pilot of an Imperial Japanese Navy torpedo bomber, hauled his heavily laden aircraft off the flight deck of the flagship Akagi and headed south towards his target: ships of the US Pacific fleet anchored at Pearl Harbour. His was the first of 353 planes, a mix of torpedo bombers, dive bombers, conventional bombers and fighters, that struggled up into the early morning sky off the decks of six aircraft carriers steaming 230 miles north of Oahu island in the American Hawaiian group. Behind his pilot, Lieutenant Commander Mitsuo Fuchida, the mission commander, sat in the observer's seat of the aircraft. At 7:53 am, by now over Oahu, Fuchida ordered his pilot to send the radio signal 'To Ra' to the Akagi, signifying that the attack was about to commence and that the Americans appeared to have been caught completely unawares. ['To Ra' comes from the initial syllables of totsugeki raigeki, meaning 'torpedo attack'. Hollywood's 20th Century Fox, depicting the events of that day, called their film Tora! Tora! Tora!]

At about 8:00 am, the first bombs and torpedoes dropped from the planes to begin their destructive journey towards the massed ships below. For the next two hours, aircrews unleashed an unrelenting bombardment on ships, planes and military installations with little resistance from the surprised Americans. Shortly before 10:00 am, work done, the last plane turned away from the island and headed back towards its mother carrier, leaving unimaginable devastation below.

The Americans had paid an appalling price. The attack had sunk or seriously damaged twenty-one ships including all eight battleships then in harbour; had destroyed 188 aircraft and damaged a further 159, the majority hit before they could take off to defend the island. 2,403 Americans including sixty-eight civilians lay dead, and a further 1,178 military personnel and civilians sustained injuries. By comparison, the Japanese Navy suffered few casualties: twenty-nine planes and their crews, less than ten per cent of the attacking force, failed to return to the carriers. But, by good fortune, America's three aircraft carriers of their Pacific fleet based at Pearl Harbour were not there. One was in dock at San Diego, California, and the other two were at sea.

The next day, in a speech to Congress, President Franklin Delano Roosevelt said of 7 December that it was 'a date which will live in infamy...' On that same day, America and Britain formally declared war on Japan. Three days later, on 11 December, Germany and Italy escalated the world conflict by declaring war on the United States. This perhaps rash act by the axis powers in Europe shifted America's covert support of the United Kingdom into an active alliance, and full participation in the European theatre of WWII. In retrospect, the axis powers' action may be considered to have sealed Germany's ultimate fate.

The Japanese attack triggered a chain of events that over the next three and a half years would forever change the lives of many million American servicemen and women scattered all over the world and their families at home, together with millions of the United Kingdom's citizens. Some Americans would never return to their homeland; others would return with physical and mental scars from which they and their families would never recover.

The friendly invasion

The leaders of the Allied nations fighting the war against Germany knew that its ultimate defeat could be accomplished only by a land battle fought on mainland Europe. With most of Europe under German occupation, they also knew that troops and equipment needed to complete that task, Russia aside, could be launched only from the United Kingdom. The forces of the UK, Commonwealth countries and European allies alone could not accomplish the task, so the might of America would be needed to provide men, women, equipment and other war supplies. Moreover, to prepare the invasion force that would eventually cross the English Channel to land on French beaches, American forces would need to train in the United Kingdom alongside their allies. So, from spring 1942, a trickle of American servicemen and women arrived in the UK that, by the end of May 1944, would be a flood, their numbers finally exceeding 1.5 million. The official code name given to the British–US plan for the reception and accommodation of US military forces in the UK in preparation for continental operations was BOLERO, but it was commonly referred to in the UK as the 'Friendly Invasion'.

The geographical relationships of America and the UK logically determined that entry into the United Kingdom for American troops and supplies crossing the Atlantic Ocean would be through its principal west coast seaports. By far the most suitable of these were on the Rivers Clyde, Mersey and Severn, and on the Welsh coast of the Bristol Channel. By May 1944, a little over fifty per cent of American personnel arrived at the Scottish River Clyde ports of Greenock, Gourock and Glasgow, and another thirty per cent at River Mersey ports, principally Liverpool. The greatest tonnage of war materials arrived at Severn and Bristol Channel ports, mainly Swansea, Cardiff, Newport and Avonmouth; and at the Mersey ports of Liverpool, Garston and Birkenhead, and Manchester via the ship canal. These two groups of ports, particularly those on the Severn and Bristol Channel, specialized in freight handling rather than passengers. By May 1944, they accounted for approximately seventy per cent of all war supplies arriving in the United Kingdom destined for American military use. The Clyde ports, by comparison, accounted for only about eight per cent of the total US tonnage discharged in the United Kingdom by the same date.

To a large extent, American entry into the UK through its west coast ports influenced the disposition of its ground forces' training in the UK. To minimise cross traffic clashes on the UK's strained railway and road systems, an early, astute decision of the Bolero committee was to concentrate American ground forces chiefly in a western triangle, with its base stretching from Cornwall to the Isle of Wight, and its apex just north of Cheltenham in Gloucestershire. British, Commonwealth and other ground forces would be based in and trained to the east of this triangle. Moreover, an excellent railway network linked Glasgow, Liverpool and the West Country, so troops entering the UK through the northern ports could be readily transferred by train to bases in the south and west despite the system being worked to capacity. By comparison, ports at which war supplies entered the UK were located much nearer to concentrations of US ground troops so the transfer of supplies by road and rail was achieved reasonably speedily.

From the disposition of their ground forces, logic dictated that American sea-borne troops would land in France on the right flank on beaches codenamed Omaha and Utah while British, Commonwealth and other nations' troops would land to the Americans' left on beaches codenamed Sword, Juno and Gold.

The need for new hospitals

Introducing over one million additional servicemen and women from the United States into the UK and the inevitable need for occasional medical treatment meant that existing facilities would be inadequate since, in 1942, British hospitals had little spare capacity. Moreover, in the period leading up to the invasion of France, British, Commonwealth and other nations' men and women in training in the UK would outnumber Americans. And many of these, in addition to the forty-eight million resident civilians, would from time to time require beds in the already overstretched existing hospitals. Unquestionably, while training for the forthcoming land battle on mainland Europe, American forces would sustain many casualties due to accidents and general sickness. Furthermore, many more men would become casualties once the land battle on mainland Europe started.

Even before the Japanese attack on Pearl Harbour, the United States expected eventually to become involved in the European war, and secret planning for American soldiers to be provided with medical facilities in the United Kingdom had been ongoing for a number of years prior to 6 June 1944. The first medical planner sent to England by the American Surgeon General's office was Colonel Paul R Hawley, who arrived in mid-September 1941. Initially working in London, Hawley set about formulating plans for dealing with American casualties once America entered

General Paul R Hawley (AMEDD)

the European war. In July 1942, he was officially appointed to the position of Chief Surgeon for the European Theatre of Operations (ETO) and, as part of the Services of Supply (SOS), set up his headquarters at Cheltenham, Gloucestershire. [After 6 June 1944, the SOS changed its designation to Communications Zone (COMZ).]

Without delay, after arriving in the UK, Hawley and his team of advisers set about the challenging task of estimating hospital bed requirements. With only World War I experience to guide them, they concluded that beds needed for sick and non-battle casualties training in the United Kingdom would be four per cent of total troop strength, this number increasing to seven per cent with the addition of battle casualties after the invasion started. To cater for these numbers, therefore, Hawley announced in June 1943 that he required 90,000 to 95,000 hospital beds to be ready for use by April 1944. British authorities made available for American use six existing hospitals as a stopgap, but this number would provide nowhere near the numbers of beds to meet America's needs. Consequently, construction immediately started that would, by D-Day, provide the Americans with 108 mixed-function hospitals in the UK. But even this number of hospitals would not provide sufficient beds to fully meet Hawley's target. Accordingly, additional beds were provided in tented extensions to wards in many general hospitals so that, by the end of 1944, close to 130,000 beds were available.

Hawley considered that about half of the required bed spaces would be needed in the build-up to the invasion to treat soldiers wounded in training, and those suffering from everyday ailments. The American designation for this type of hospital was a 'Station Hospital', designed to accommodate 750 bed patients. Following the invasion, many of these hospitals would become redundant. Therefore, a number of them, including Tyntesfield, were upgraded prior to the invasion to notionally accommodate 1,000 bed patients. The 1,000-bed hospitals, primarily to care for battle casualties, were designated 'General Hospitals'. In practice, as built to British specifications, a 750-bed station hospital actually provided 834 beds while a 1,000-bed general hospital provided 1,082 beds.

Hawley ideally wanted one station hospital to be sited within every divisional training area of about 25,000 men and within about five miles of the centre of a troop concentration. Moreover, Hawley and his team decided that, when battle casualties started to arrive following the invasion of France, the most rapid and comfortable means of transferring them from near-port early treatment hospitals to general hospitals farther inland would be by train. Therefore, an additional prerequisite was that inland hospitals should be situated close to adequate railway stations, and on track networks that would provide straightforward access for hospital trains from the south coast without unduly disrupting overall rail traffic flow. Armed with Hawley's brief, the British War Office and Ministry of Agriculture set about locating suitable sites for hospitals, concentrating on parklands or estates to avoid building on farmland so essential for food production.

By the end of 1943, Bristol, North Somerset and South Gloucestershire had become home to one of the largest concentrations of American servicemen and women in the UK, with more than twenty-five camps and supply depots. Bristol itself housed the headquarters of the First US Army at Clifton College, and also America's largest general materials storage depot in the UK. This depot, set up in July 1942, eventually comprised fourteen separate installations in 200 different buildings, spread over a large part of Bristol itself and the immediately surrounding countryside, and staffed by many thousands of men and women. Additionally, at Bristol's Avonmouth docks, where ships regularly arrived with food, petrol and war materials from the United States, a large contingent of American dockworkers played a leading role in unloading their nation's ships.

The Tyntesfield Park Estate, owned by Lady Wraxall, therefore, approximately seven miles by road from Bristol with its mainline railway facilities and a generally adequate road system, satisfied all criteria. So, in the autumn of 1942, the War Office requisitioned approximately fifty acres of land on which to build a hospital for the American army.

Colonel Hawley preferably wanted his hospitals in the UK to be built by US army engineers to specifications and plans drawn up by the American Surgeon General's department using materials and equipment shipped over from the States. But, in mid-1942, with ships in the Atlantic convoys heading for the UK loaded with essential food equipment, and petroleum products being sunk by German submarines, cargo space was at a premium. Wise man that he was, Hawley knew that taking up space in ships to transport materials from the States for hospital construction in the UK would never be permitted. Reluctantly, therefore, he agreed to all the hospitals being constructed by British civilian contractors, to British designs and specifications prepared by the country's Ministry of Works, using British materials, and fitted out mostly with British equipment.

To the Americans, British standards of hospital accommodation were lower in many respects than their own. The Ministry of Works resisted demands for higher standards requiring more labour and better construction materials simply because neither was readily available. Each change in specification requested by the Americans became the subject of hard bargaining. The Americans won on floor space allocation for each bed – 72 sq ft compared with the British norm of 60 sq ft. They achieved larger bathing facilities than the British norm and, critically, they had their way on operating suite design and equipment. But the MOW would not improve the standards of kitchen space and equipment, nor on the methods of heating buildings.

However, Hawley uncompromisingly insisted that certain facilities be provided. He demanded that a pure water supply be available at all times, and that hospital sewage be properly discharged and treated. And he also demanded that dual 110 and 230 volt electric wiring and fittings be installed since Americans insisted on using some of their own specialised equipment that operated on the lower voltage, particularly surgical and medical that was shipped over from the United States. However, despite the concessions on some standards won so grudgingly from the MOW, overall, the Americans still considered the accommodation and facilities austere and, in some ways, primitive.

Planning and construction

In early November 1942, local people travelling along the B3130 Long Ashton to Wraxall road would no doubt have cast inquisitive glances at the earth-moving machines, cranes, concrete mixers and huts that had appeared in a field at the bottom of the Tyntesfield estate. The workers on the estate, the drinkers in the pubs and clubs, and the shoppers in the local towns and villages all, no doubt, held opinions about what was going on. Some, who considered themselves to be 'in the know', would tap the side of their nose with a forefinger, and wink to indicate their exclusive knowledge. But no clues as to what was going on were officially revealed. Even the announcement at the Long Ashton Rural District Council meeting held on 24 November

1942 was delivered in somewhat vague terms. A minute records the Clerk's statement to the meeting:

Some members of the committee are no doubt aware that a large Government contract has been commenced in Tyntesfield Park near Flax Bourton station, the premises being erected are specially needed to assist the war effort, and have to be finished in a very quick time. Large numbers of men will be employed, and there is great need for them to be housed as near as possible to their work. If voluntary billets are not forthcoming, compulsion will have to be used to make people accommodate them.

No later reference appears in the council's minute book, so presumably local householders, either willingly or reluctantly, found sufficient accommodation for the workers.

The land the War Office requisitioned from Lady Wraxall for the hospital formed roughly the shape of a right-angled triangle and occupied approximately fifty acres. The base of the triangle, about 700 yards long, followed the B3130 road, and its 500-yard shortest side projected north-east up into the wooded estate. The site was mostly level away from the entrance, but then sloped gently up into the estate. The only vehicular access into the hospital was from the narrow Wraxall road, and locals insist that, to form this access, the longest holly hedge in England was breached.

The identity of the main contractor cannot be established with certainty. Recollections of some local people who remembered the hospital being built insist that Robert McAlpine carried out the work. This company did indeed build a number of American hospitals during WWII as did Alfred McAlpine, George Wimpey and others. Or it might possibly have been a Bristol building contractor, capable of constructing such a project.

At this stage of the war, British contractors were constructing many hospitals for both British and American use, and completion target dates were rarely achieved. Many reasons contributed to the lateness of completion: shortage of labour, particularly in the skilled categories required for this specialist type of project; shortage of materials and inconsistent deliveries; short daylight hours during winter months; and, bizarrely in time of war, working hours limited by union regulations during summer months.

Building a hospital was a considerably more complex undertaking than building a barracks or a warehouse. Exacting attention had to be given to installing special electrical and plumbing fixtures, telephone lines and switchboards, steam boilers, and high-pressure hot-water autoclaves to sterilise surgical instruments and other equipment. Although no figures are available for Tyntesfield, construction of hospitals elsewhere in the UK employed up to about 450 workers, with a tight construction programme of seven months.

The hospital buildings and environment

When completed, the hospital would initially accommodate 834 bed patients and 680 hospital staff. As a self-sufficient hospital, it would need specifically designated and equipped buildings to house many different departments: an operating suite, post-operative surgical wards, recovery wards, medical wards, out-patients clinic and dispensary, headquarters and other office buildings, a pharmacy, a dental clinic, a mortuary, stores, chapel, a motor pool, officers' and nurses' quarters, enlisted men's barracks, ablutions blocks, kitchen and mess facilities, recreation rooms, and a host of other buildings for a miscellany of functions. In total, 103 buildings would be erected.

To a large extent and wherever practical, buildings were prefabricated in sections in factories elsewhere in the UK. Although no details are available, the sectional buildings would most likely have been transported by rail to Flax Bourton or other nearby railway stations, taken on lorries by road to site, and assembled into complete buildings. Local quarries provided materials for building roads and other hardstand areas, while concrete for foundations and floor slabs, and mortar for brickwork were mixed on site. Local haulage companies were used as much as possible, and labour would mostly have been drawn from nearby and from Bristol.

All buildings on the complex were single storey. Ward buildings were of a standard layout but varied in length and accommodation provided. A typical thirty-bed ward building measured 140 ft long by 25 ft 6 in wide, its main open ward being approximately 71 ft long by 24 ft wide. At the rear double-door entrance end, terracotta brick walls subdivided the building to provide a nurses' office, a kitchen, separate dirty and clean linen rooms, a sluice room, a doctor's office/examination room, lavatories, patient's clothing room, and two private rooms, all rooms accessed off a central corridor.

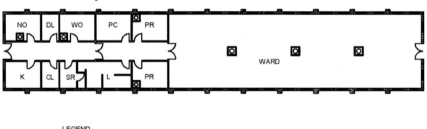

LEGEND

NO - NURSES OFFICE	PC - PATIENTS CLOTHING	CL - CLEAN LINEN
DL - DIRTY LINEN	PR - PRIVATE ROOM FOR	SR - SLUICE ROOM
WO - WARD OFFICER/	SERIOUSLY ILL PATIENT	L - LAVATORY
EXAMINATION ROOM	K - KITCHEN	◙ STOVE

TYPICAL THIRTY BED WARD

Scale

*Typical ward layout prepared from an original sketch
in the 56th GH records (Author and 56th GH records – NARA)*

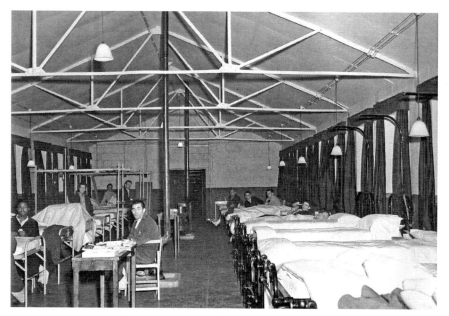

Typical recovery ward. (56th GH records – NARA)

The central corridor continued through to the main unpartitioned open ward area where fifteen beds were spaced along both outside walls, with just sufficient room between beds to accommodate a small locker.

The operating suite building was accessed through a double doorway midway along the long side facing the surgical wards, the doors opening onto a lobby that in turn linked with a full-length central corridor. The suite provided two operating rooms, one at each end of the building, each equipped with two operating tables. Mains lights to illuminate the tables were backed up by battery-operated lights and standby generators so that, if mains power failed, operations could proceed uninterrupted. The building also contained two smaller operating rooms for minor surgery, a resuscitation room, an instrument room, an anaesthesia room, a plastering room, and offices, toilets, etc, all accessed off the main corridor.

A number of different building forms were used in the hospital. All wards, the operating suite and administration buildings were of robust construction, while personnel accommodation and other minor buildings were generally of timber-framed construction. In the more robustly constructed buildings, ground floor concrete slabs were laid with integral pockets formed in them at their long edges, at approximately 12 ft spacing. Into these pockets, precast concrete columns were located and their lower ends rigidly concreted in to form a stable column. In one form of building, prefabricated steel roof trusses were bolted to the column tops, and in a second type, precast concrete roof beams were similarly bolted to the columns. In

Aerial photograph of the camp taken by RAF on 4 December 1946. (English Heritage – NMR)

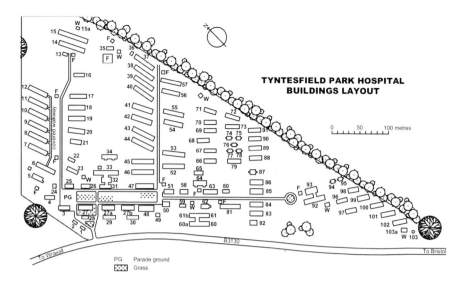

TYNTESFIELD PARK HOSPITAL BUILDINGS LAYOUT

0   50   100 metres

PG   Parade ground
░░░   Grass

The buildings functions are those given in 56th GH reports.

1 Unit Supply Office
2 Carpenter's Shop
3 Chapel
4 Morgue
5 Boiler House – Central Supply
6 Operating Suite
7-12 Surgical Wards
13-15 VD Section
15a Water Tower
16 Isolation Ward
17-20 Wards
21 Laboratory
22 EENT Clinic
23 X-ray – Physical Therapy
24 Transformer House
25 Dental Clinic
26 Receiving & Information Office
27 Headquarters
27a Registrar and Detachment of Patients
27b D.C.R.E
28 Motor Pool
29-30 Medical Supply Warehouses
31-33 Patients' Mess Hall
34 Patients' Recreation Hall
35 Boiler House
36 Mental Ward
37-46 Wards
47 Patients' Baggage Room
48 Medical Supply Office and Warehouse
49 Post Exchange
50 Firehouse
51 Pharmacy

52-57 Wards
58 Office of Medical And Surgical Services
59 Mailroom, Barbers Shop and Tailor
60-61 Officers' Quarters
60a Unit Supply Warehouse
61a Mess Warehouse
62 Officers' Latrine
63 Enlisted Men's Cookhouse
64 Enlisted Men's Mess Hall
65-73 Enlisted Men's Barracks
74 Enlisted Men's Ablution
75 Enlisted Men's Shower Room
76 Enlisted Men's Latrine
77 Enlisted Men's Ablution
78 Enlisted Men's Shower Room
79 Enlisted Men's Barracks
80 Detachment Office
81 Officers' Club
82-84 Officers' Quarters
85-86 Enlisted Men's Barracks
87 Ablution
88-91 Enlisted Men's Barracks
92 Officers' Mess Hall
93 Officers' Cookhouse
94 Nurses' Latrine
95 Nurses' Ablution and Showers
96-102 Nurses' Quarters
103 Pump House
103a Reserve Water Supply Tank
W Static Water Tank
F Fuel Bin

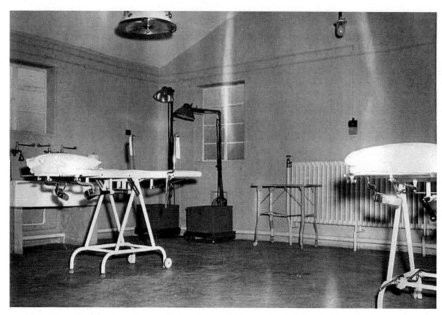

Operating suite Brickbarns Farm, Melvern. Tyntesfield was identical. (56th GH records – NARA)

both building types, asbestos cement corrugated sheets provided a watertight roof, and plasterboard sheets, following the roof slope, formed a ceiling. Walls of terracotta bricks, incorporating windows and doors, were built between the concrete columns to create windproof, watertight walls. Buildings to house hospital personnel, and some other minor buildings, comprised wholly timber-framed prefabricated structures bolted onto a concrete floor slab. Internally, walls and the roof were lined with plasterboard sheets, and externally with sheets of a waterproof 'rubberised' type of material. As on the ward buildings, asbestos cement corrugated sheets clad the roof. Unlike most other hospitals under construction for the Americans elsewhere in the UK at the time, no Nissen or Quonsett buildings were used at Tyntesfield.

To indicate to enemy aircraft that the site was a hospital, ward buildings displayed large red crosses on their roofs though, at time of opening, the Luftwaffe rarely appeared in the skies of the West Country.

With only one exception, solid-fuel 'pot-bellied' stoves, commonly called 'tortoise' stoves, burning low-grade coal or coke, heated all buildings throughout the hospital complex. In total over 400 of these 'pot-bellied' stoves were installed. The one exception was the operating suite which was heated by hot-water radiators. In a typical ward building, three of the 'pot-bellied' stoves heated the thirty-bed main ward while smaller stoves heated four of the ancillary rooms. The number of stoves provided in other buildings was related to the building's size: for example, two stoves heated the open-plan nurses' quarters.

At design stage, the Ministry of Works specified that all ward floors in newly constructed hospitals in the UK were to be covered with linoleum. This type of floor finish could be cleaned easily, vital for both appearance and hygiene. But the contractor took little care in finishing the concrete floor surface expecting that linoleum would later be laid onto the concrete. It turned out, however, that linoleum was in such short supply that sufficient quantities could not be obtained for the whole UK hospital construction programme, so the concrete floors left by the contractor had to do. Typically, however, and those at Tyntesfield were no exception, floor surfaces were not level, of rough finish, crumbled easily, forever created large amounts of dust when swept, and damaged delicate equipment that was wheeled over it. In short, the floors were totally unsuitable for a hospital.

Hawley, by now promoted to the rank of general, insisted that the Ministry of Works quickly come up with an answer to the floor problem. After much experimenting with different materials, they eventually came up with a solution. This was to lay on the concrete floors a 3/4-inch thick layer of pitch mastic, a synthetic black material similar to road surfacing material used today. In a hot plastic form, the mastic could be readily spread and trowelled level, and, after cooling, it congealed into a hard, smooth mass. Finally, the surface was waxed to provide a highly polished floor that could easily be swept and cleaned. However, in use there were drawbacks: the surface showed every scratch and dust particle, it softened in the areas of heating stoves, and bed legs and other heavy furniture readily sank into it unless the load from the leg was spread using timber plates.

Unidentified nurse in front of one of the nurses' quarters. (Winston Hawkins)

Road construction within the complex was a mix of concrete and rolled hardcore, with footpaths similarly constructed using the same mix of materials. The entrance off the public highway into the hospital complex, all roads around the motor pool, the parade ground, the lower-level road off the parade ground running past the headquarters building, and the higher-level road off the parade ground running past the patients' mess hall were all constructed using concrete. In the vicinity of the firehouse and the pharmacy, the higher and lower roads converged into a single road that terminated in a roundabout close to the officers' mess hall. This last single road and two other roads that accessed ward buildings were less robustly constructed using rolled hardcore.

Water supply and sewage disposal

To provide a water supply and sewerage system for 680 hospital staff and 834 patients – this number would increase after the invasion of France to more than 1,300 at times – was not an insubstantial problem. Although the quantity of water used at peak times in the hospital is not known, an indication can be gained from the fact that the sewage treatment plant was designed to treat approximately 55,000 gallons of sewage each day.

Bristol Waterworks Company supplied mains water to the hospital complex from deep-bore wells at their abstraction plant at Chelvey, just over four miles south-west of the hospital. At the plant, the water was chlorinated and treated to drinkable quality before being piped to the hospital where it entered the site at the most south-easterly point close to the nurses' quarters. From here, it was pumped along the eastern edge of the site and stored in a 24,000-gallon high-level steel tank housed in a tower at the highest point on the site. From this elevated tank, water flowed in buried pipes to where required. Although no details are available about the construction of the water tower, similar structures at other hospital sites were often one hundred feet high, built in reinforced concrete and clad in brickwork.

Also at the point of entry to the site, a buried 34,000-gallon concrete reservoir maintained a reserve supply. Water was pumped from this reservoir to the tower tank when required so that it was always full. In addition, five uncovered ground-level water tanks, each containing 10,000 gallons, maintained a supply for firefighting and emergency use. Regular bacteriological analysis in the hospital laboratory always found the water quality to be satisfactory, albeit 'hard'.

The sewage treatment plant, operated by a civilian contractor, was located approximately 500 yards south-west of the hospital adjacent to what is now known as Bathing Pond Wood, on what was then Gable Farm. Sewage from the hospital flowed by gravity through six-inch buried pipes where it was processed at the plant. The plant comprised sedimentation tanks, percolation filters, humus tanks, and sludge-drying beds; and the liquid effluent was piped to a nearby stream that ultimately discharged into the River Yeo. The sediment in the settlement tanks was periodically reclaimed and used as fertiliser on the land.

But, in operation, the sewage disposal provisions, both in the hospital and at the sewerage plant, did not always perform well. British-designed plumbing and grease traps connected to mechanical dishwashers could not always cope with the unusually large amounts of fats present in American

Water tower at Kington, Herefordshire, home to the US 107th GH in 1944. This tower was typical of the type built for hospitals and other military establishments in WWII. (Ken Reeves, Kington Museum)

foods. And, at the disposal plant, fats in the liquid waste clogged filter beds, the mess occasionally spilling over onto adjacent land. Large quantities of sawdust from nearby sawmills were periodically spread to mop up the spills, later to be spread onto farmland as fertiliser.

When construction work neared completion, and in line with agreed policy between the American Chief Surgeon's office, the British War Office and the Ministry of Works, an American advance party moved in midway through September 1943. The advance party comprised Detachment A, formed at the 298th General Hospital Headquarters at Frenchay, three miles north of Bristol. The role of this detachment, comprising one officer and fifteen enlisted men, was to guard the hospital and help set it up so that, when the assigned medical unit arrived, the hospital would be fully equipped and ready.

With the advance party resident, the British Army delivered basic items necessary to enable the hospital to function: beds, kitchen equipment, firefighting equipment (fire pumps, water buckets, stirrup pumps, etc), office equipment (desks and chairs, filing cabinets, typewriters, telephones, etc) and many other miscellaneous items. The Americans supplied additional equipment to bring the facility up to their higher standard. They also provided most of the surgical equipment used in the operating suite since they were more familiar with its use than similar equipment standard in British hospitals. The British provided other less technical equipment.

Chapter Three

Nurses, Red Cross and 'Holy Joes'

While the surgeon, using his skill, experience and dedication, repaired broken bodies and sustained life in his patients, those who nursed them, particularly the female nurses, provided immeasurable post-operative care and comfort. They went out of their way to make GIs feel safe thousands of miles from home in the most appalling situations. [GI refers to an American soldier or his equipment – from initial letters of **G**overnment **I**ssue.]

Mary Roberts in her book 'American Nursing: History and Interpretation', wrote:

> *A hypodermic for pain could be quickly given, but reassuring a suffering patient and helping him to decide how he would break the news of his extensive injury to his family or sweetheart required more time. As they flew from bed to bed, sensitive nurses were keenly aware of the patient's unspoken need for reassurance.*

And an unidentified American General said:

> *I say in all sincerity that no one has done more for the American soldier than the nurses in our hospitals. The patient makes faster progress when a nurse looks after them. She's an American woman who represents home, mother, wife and sister to the wounded soldier. Just the sound of her voice sometimes is as good as medicine.*

Many of the nurses joined the American Army Nursing Corps straight from training hospitals. They all started their army careers with the rank of second lieutenant because the army felt that 'officer rank' gave them some degree of protection against over-amorous enlisted men. [Enlisted men were below officer or warrant officer ranks.]

In both units that would reside at Tyntesfield, the 56th and 74th General Hospitals, nurses were allocated separately to surgical and medical departments, but periodically spent time in the receiving office, EENT [eyes, ears, nose and throat] clinic, and in the central supply office. All nursing staff served under the direct supervision of a chief nurse and an assistant chief nurse. Nurses on the wards generally worked a twelve-hour day shift from 7:00 am to 7:00 pm, and a night shift covering the other twelve-hour period, usually in three-week stints, with time for meals and rest snatched whenever they could.

In practice, the head nurse managed the day-to-day running of each ward with as many other nurses as patient-load and supervision of some enlisted men demanded. When America entered WWII, its army regulations stipulated that female nurses must be between the ages of twenty-one and forty. But, as the war progressed, the shortage of good nurses became a problem as demand increased. Consequently, the age limit was raised to forty-five. But even this did not completely meet the demand for nurses in both the European and Pacific theatres of war. Therefore, enlisted men, trained in medical schools as medical technicians, increasingly assisted nurses with some of their duties on the wards.

Some nurses, in addition to their normal duties, spent time instructing medical technicians about the nursing role: how to take a patient's temperature, blood pressure and pulse, give a bed bath, and make beds. Mostly, nurses gave injections and medication, and set up blood transfusions and drips, but, at times of high chaos, the brightest, most dependable male technicians helped out with this work. And the lowest ranks of enlisted men usually got the dirty jobs. Among others, they cleaned up vomit and excrement, a duty, it is said, that some nurses considered not befitting an officer. Bizarrely, however, in compliance with American Army law at the time, only females could be enlisted into the Army Nurse Corps and be called a 'nurse', so medical technicians who performed this role could not technically carry that title.

In the operating suite, four nurses, each working a twelve-hour shift, cared for patients on the two tables in each operating room. They assisted the surgeons with surgical procedures: handing surgical instruments to them, suturing and applying dressings, etc. And some who had undergone training as anaesthetists performed that role too.

Also in the operating suite, surgeons and nurses were ably supported by enlisted men who had undergone special training as surgical technicians in army medical schools in the United States. Their main role was doing the 'heavy' work: helping nurses to transfer a patient from a litter onto the operating table, and generally preparing him for surgery. They also cleaned up the operating rooms and tables after an operation, sterilized equipment and restocked the room between operations, made plaster casts and splints, and applied plaster of Paris to limbs. And, at times of high pressure, the most competent of the male technicians also performed the role of nurse in assisting the surgeons.

74th General Hospital Red Cross workers – identities unknown. (Tracey Brake – niece of Robert Thiessen)

American Red Cross workers

Although not strictly part of the nursing service, the all-female Red Cross workers attached to both the 56th and 74th GHs provided a supplementary yet indispensable welfare service. In both hospital units, the Red Cross contingent comprised two social workers, two recreation workers, and a secretary-accountant although, later in their residence, the 56th employed a sixth as an additional secretary. Although the roles of the first two pairs of workers appear fairly clear-cut, at times the distinction blurred. They regularly visited wards, distributing 'goodies' such as playing cards, newspapers, magazines, books and stationery. And when patients who had been wounded in battle arrived, Red Cross workers provided simple comfort articles such as pocket combs, toothbrushes and shaving equipment, all of which most soldiers had lost on the beaches and in the countryside of the Continent. They also spent considerable time talking to patients regarding future planning of their lives, particularly those with amputations.

For administrative purposes, the Red Cross workers were classed as US Army officers with a nominal rank of second lieutenant. Responsible to the chief nurse, they lived in the nurses' quarters and observed their army rules and regulations. They dressed in similar uniforms to the nurses, but also wore a distinguishing white armband bearing a red cross. They observed the nurses' rules regarding times to return to living quarters at night; and times away from duty, such as pleasure trips and generally time off base. And like the nurses, they could not be seen to openly fraternize with enlisted men.

Hospital personnel responsible for patients quickly recognized that boredom was a major obstacle to recovery, and, to some extent, also to the happiness of the hospital staff. Soon after the 56th General Hospital established its headquarters at Tyntesfield, the first unit to take up residence, American Red Cross workers attached to the hospital converted a small spare ward – building 34 – into a recreation hall for patients. They equipped the open area of the ward with ping-pong [table tennis] tables, a billiard table, dartboards, a piano, radio, record player and table games. They also set up a library with a varied selection of books, magazines and American newspapers. All of these items were regularly taken around the wards on carts for the bed-bound patients. They converted the kitchen of the ward into a craft and carpenter shop organised and run by patients with skills in those occupations. Encouraged and helped by the Red Cross workers, patients made articles for themselves and useful items of equipment for the wards.

For those patients confined to bed because of the nature of their injuries – many with severe leg injuries were in traction – the Red Cross obtained a movie projector so that films could be shown in the wards. A regular, changing supply of films was available throughout the American hospitals' organisation in the UK. Ambulatory patients were also able to view the films either by visiting the wards, or in their recreation hall.

The Red Cross also organised various types of group recreation: musical recitals, community singing, bingo parties, quizzes, etc. Prizes, purchased through the Red Cross fund, were awarded to make the competitive spirit keener. Whenever possible, talent from the local community and visits from mostly American entertainers, provided through the USO [United Service Organization], visited the hospital to provide variety. However, there is no record that any of the top stars – Bob Hope, Glen Miller, Bing Crosby, etc ever visited the hospital. And although some local people insist that General Eisenhower paid a visit to Tyntesfield, no official record can be located to confirm this.

When a patient arrived at the hospital, the military authorities automatically notified families back home in the United States that their son or daughter had been wounded or injured and was in hospital in the UK. As well as the official notification to a relative, a hospital Red Cross social worker discussed with the patient whether he wanted his family to know more about the nature of his injuries. If he agreed but was unable to write a letter, the hospital worker wrote it for him, subject to the approval of his doctor, the hospital commanding officer and the military censor. The social worker endeavoured to assure relatives that excellent doctors and surgeons were caring for their loved one, and that they would receive the best individual care possible.

Although American Red Cross workers provided the essential welfare services, two army chaplains – commonly referred to as 'Holy Joes' – one

Roman Catholic and one Protestant, contributed immensely to the well–being of patients and hospital staff in both the 56th and 74th. In addition to holding regular religious services in the hospital chapel, they also worked tirelessly in providing a ready ear to both patients and members of the hospital team who wanted to discuss personal problems. Their role, therefore, extended beyond the purely ecclesiastical mission into the welfare and social work roles. The chaplains also distributed Purple Hearts and other medals to patients. [The Purple Heart medal was awarded to all American servicemen injured in battle.] An officer of the Jewish faith occasionally held services on the base, and also arranged for Jewish staff to attend services in the civilian community nearby.

The Post Exchange on the hospital, while not strictly classed as a 'welfare service', also provided a most important social service to all hospital personnel.

Chapter Four

The 56th General Hospital

The first medical unit to take up permanent residence and run the hospital was the 56th General Hospital. It was formally activated in February 1941, but effectively in name only. For the next two years, the unit operated almost exclusively in a training role at Carlisle Barracks, Pennsylvania. Qualified doctors, after receiving their commissions in the Medical Corps, were sent to Medical Field Service Schools, one of which was at Carlisle Barracks. Here, they received preliminary training in army medical practices, some within the 56th GH unit. But, three times over the next two years, Medical Corps authorities transferred many fully trained doctors out of the 56th to newly formed hospital units to assist with their training.

But then, in May 1943, the 56th role was about to change. Lieutenant Colonel Daniel S Sheehan, commanding officer of the 56th GH, together with two other doctors, was ordered to Fort Jackson, South Carolina, to prepare the unit for overseas service. Other medical personnel and nurses were assigned to the unit, and Lt Col Sheehan scoured the army's medical training schools to obtain outstanding enlisted men. During July 1943, the 56th's officers, nurses and enlisted men received further training at Fort Jackson's two station hospitals. In addition to the normal medical training of a hospital unit, all personnel received special training in setting up and operating a tented hospital. To the more perceptive members of the unit, this could only be for one purpose: the unit would either transfer to North Africa or be ready to transfer to France to operate a forward hospital near to the battle lines once the fighting in France started.

After numerous redeployments within the United States, further training and much uncertainty as to their overseas destination, in early October 1943, they received the orders they had been waiting for and headed for Boston harbour. The uncertainty and waiting was finally over and the 56th General Hospital, comprising fifty-six officers, one hundred nurses, five hundred enlisted men and five female Red Cross workers boarded the British liner *Mauretania*. On 9 October 1943, the ship set sail. At the time of sailing, none of the hospital personnel knew where the ship was heading, but a few days into the voyage they learnt that the unit was not going to North Africa but to England.

Left: *56th GH enlisted men's lapel pin. (Martin Collins)*

Below left: *56th GH CO Lt. Col. Daniel Sheehan. (Molly Placko)*

Above: *Winston Hawkins at right of group. Other soldiers, location and date unknown. (Winston Hawkins)*

Left: *RMS Mauretania that brought the 56th GH to England.*

Like all the pre-war luxury liners converted as troop carriers, the *Mauretania* sailed alone, relying on averaging a speed close to twenty-six knots and a continually changing course to outwit U-boat crews. And, like all peacetime liners converted to the role of troop carrier, the number of passengers was five to six times the number for which the ship had been designed. On this particular voyage, the *Mauretania* carried 9,000 passengers in addition to its crew.

One of the soldiers heading for England was Private Benjamin Dangerfield III, a twenty-one year-old who had been trained by the army as a clerk. He recalls the voyage:

> *Our quarters were many, many decks below as the upper decks were reserved for the officers and nurses. We had a choice of sleeping on a flat bunk or a hammock, and I chose a hammock. We were in a big room with a washroom/shower room adjacent. As soon as I could I climbed the many stairs up to the upper deck to watch us sail out of Boston Harbor. I always went up to one of the top decks, bringing with me a paperback book and a crossword puzzle and only went below for meals. Lots of the guys were seasick because they stayed below, but I never got seasick.*

And Winston Hawkins, a twenty-two year-old staff sergeant also recalls aspects of the trip:

> *As I remember the weather was good. The officers were housed on the upper decks and enlisted men lower. I was on D deck and we slept on our coats on the deck floor. I remember being it was a British ship that the crew was British. We were served orange marmalade put on the table in gallon cans. To this day it is still something that I do not have a desire for. As I remember it was a smooth trip although the unknown made for an apprehensive trip.*

After nine days at sea, on 18 October 1943, the *Mauretania* tied up at Liverpool docks.

England

Before their involvement in the war, many of the men and women who disembarked from the ship, and many less than twenty years old, had never ventured outside their home state, and some had never even left their home town. Their thoughts can only be imagined as they arrived at a cheerless port in a foreign country, not knowing what the future held for them. But perhaps some appreciation can be gained from the words of the chief nurse in her report 'History of Army Nursing in the 56th General Hospital' written soon after the war's end:

> *One hundred bewildered nurses, neatly dressed in Class A uniform, but loaded down with gas mask, musette bag*, pistol belt and handbag, stumbled down the gangplank, stepped out onto foreign soil and said almost in unison, "What now!"*

*[A musette bag was the American Army equivalent of today's backpack or haversack, and could hold about forty pounds weight of kit.]

On the dockside, American Red Cross women – the *doughnut dollies* – served the traditional coffee and doughnuts to the hospital's personnel. Then, following their welcome to Britain, they set off to march to nearby Lime Street station and a railway journey to the next 'destination unknown'. On the march, they witnessed first-hand the true horrors of modern warfare as they passed the ruins of shops and houses blown apart by German bombs. At the railway station, hospital personnel boarded the train that would take them to their first posting: Malvern Wells in the county of Worcestershire. The 56th's official records note that 'carriages were unlike those on American railways with a side corridor, six-person compartments, and no heating'. It was a cold and hungry group of people, therefore, that eventually arrived at Malvern Wells railway station. There, without delay, they climbed into army trucks for transfer to the hospital site.

The 56th's first posting was to the newly built hospital at Brickbarns Farm near Malvern Wells, where it was to specialise in treating neuro-psychiatric (NP) patients. When staff arrived, they were dismayed to find that the buildings still needed much work to make them useable, typical of most hospitals under construction at that time for American use. So, over the next few days, hospital personnel set to with brooms to clear away litter, with soap and water to clean up dirt, and generally make the accommodation habitable. Eventually, on 10 November 1943, the 56th officially opened as a 674-bed GH specialising in treating NP cases, and a few days later received its first patients.

However, three weeks after arriving at Malvern Wells, just as the hospital had readied itself to receive patients, about half its complement moved again. On 8 November 1943, a group comprising twenty-five officers including a chaplain, twenty-five nurses, one dietician, one physiotherapy aide and 200 enlisted men formed Detachment A of the hospital unit; its role to set up and temporarily operate a 750-bed station hospital elsewhere. Later that same day, the group left Brickbarns Farm to travel south by road to the Tyntesfield Park Estate in Somerset, about seven miles south-west of Bristol, to set about its new task.

At Tyntesfield

As at the Brickbarns Farm site, when the group arrived at Tyntesfield, construction workers were still on site, striving to complete buildings and infrastructure, while the men of Detachment A of the 298th GH from Frenchay continued with the work to install and commission equipment so vital to the hospital's primary function.

Winston Hawkins, the staff sergeant who earlier reflected on the Atlantic crossing, worked in the registrar's office. He recalls with amusement the everyday ritual of the construction workers, with their 'little tin buckets', stopping for tea at about 10:30 every morning, a ritual well recounted in a popular song from that period: 'Everything Stops for Tea'.

Although construction of the buildings according to official records had been completed before the 56th's Detachment A arrived, it was clear that much work had still to be done, particularly to the infrastructure. A prompt opening was essential so that the hospital could start to admit and treat patients from the growing troop concentrations in Bristol and its surrounding areas. Consequently, as at Brickbarns, all those who could be made available from the hospital's utilities department helped the builders speed up the work and make the site functional, and enlisted men with suitable civilian trades were immediately put to best use.

The American press presented a more embellished view of the hospital's state of readiness. On 14 March 1944, the Baltimore Sun newspaper printed an article written by one of its war correspondents, Holbrook Bradley, about

View along internal upper road towards southeast. Building 51 at far end. (Winston Hawkins)

the 56th arrival at Tyntesfield, though for security reasons the unit was not named in the article. The newspaper headed the article: 'Yank General Hospital In England Mostly Built By Staff's Own Hands'.

Somewhere in England – doctors, nurses and enlisted personnel in an army general hospital unit recently set up in Great Britain have assumed the dual capacity of medics and engineers in establishing their group in an area which a few months back was pasture land. The unit arrived at its present location some time ago, to find the bare essentials of a hospital laid out by the British. The main buildings and a few central roads had been constructed, but before full medical work could begin a great deal of additional engineering had to be undertaken.

Despite the clearly unfinished state of the hospital, the nurses particularly appeared to settle in to their new posting quite well. They were accommodated in quarters at the somewhat remote south-east end of the complex, sixteen to twenty to a building. In her war's end summary, the chief nurse reported that:

Here we had comfortable quarters in theatre of operations type buildings – a dresser for each four girls, comfortable chairs, American stoves [sic], a radio, and British-type steel cots with straw mattresses in some cases, more frequently only the bedding roll as a mattress. Our spare hours

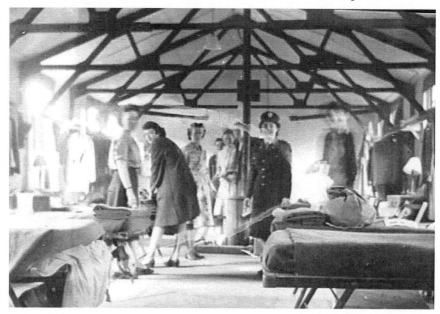

Nurses quarters, building number unknown. (Winston Hawkins)

View towards southwest with enlisted men's barracks on left. (Winston Hawkins)

were filled with letter writing, playing cards, and reading. We organised a women's officers club which was later consolidated with the men's officers club.

The male officers were housed in quarters similar to the nurses, and slept in similar individual beds. The enlisted men, however, were not so well catered for. Thirty-two men slept in a barrack building in double-decked wooden bunks. En-suite facilities were also a luxury not afforded to any of the hospital's personnel. Toilet and washing facilities were in separate buildings, relatively close to sleeping quarters, but a world away in the middle of the night in rain, snow or howling winds.

On 15 November 1943, Detachment A officially opened at Tyntesfield as a 750-bed [834 actual] station hospital. Soon thereafter, Detachment A of 298th GH returned to its duties at Frenchay hospital. At this time, although much work remained to be done, the hospital's administrators recognised that receiving and treating patients with the contractor trying to work around hospital staff was impractical and undesirable from a security viewpoint. For those reasons, the building contractor was released from further involvement, and hospital staff completed outstanding work.

With the arrival of winter, men and women of Detachment A soon discovered the shortcomings of roads that had been built by the British contractor. The rain quickly transformed the three hardcore roads within the hospital complex into quagmires since they had been constructed from

View from Wraxall road showing 56th GH's nameboard. (Molly Placko)

Main entrance taken winter 1943/ spring 1944.(Winston Hawkins

Road drainage under construction by 56th GH Utilities Department, early 1944.Building 42 nearest left. (Winston Hawkins)

crushed rock and cinders with no impervious surfacing to shed rainwater. Moving around on foot, bicycle, or by Jeep or truck required carefully negotiating mud and stagnant pools of water. So, one of the early major projects started by the utilities department was to dig trenches at both sides of the roads to drain rainwater away, and regrade the road surface to shed water into the drains. But because few personnel could be spared from their operational duties, the project moved forward slowly, and it was not until the main unit arrived on 13 January 1944 that the project gathered momentum, the work being completed by the end of March 1944.

Another shortcoming of the internal road system soon became apparent. The twelve-foot wide concrete roads did not provide sufficient width for drivers of various types of army vehicles to easily pass each other, and corners and junctions required excessive manoeuvring to negotiate. So, soon after the main hospital unit arrived, a clockwise one-way road system was introduced, and work started to further ease problems by laying new concrete areas to widen junctions and corners.

As the hospital settled into its operational role, many other improvements were implemented to improve efficiency and make life easier; most carried out by the always busy utilities department. The carpenters of the department made hundreds of timber plates to put under the legs of beds and other heavy items to spread their load and prevent them sinking into the pitch mastic that had been laid on the concrete floors. They constructed a covered walkway to link the operating suite to

surgical wards. This comprised a concrete path/roadway, roofed by asbestos/cement sheeting supported on timber cross beams and precast concrete posts set in concrete. The walkway was just wide enough to accommodate a Jeep onto which a litter could be fitted, enabling patients to be transferred from the operating suite to the post-operative surgical wards. Although open at its sides, the covered way did provide some degree of protection from the elements.

Covered walkway, location cannot positively be identified. (Winston Hawkins)

The hospital organisation

Some might argue that the doctors and nurses who cared most directly for the wounded and sick should be rated the most important people in the hospital, but without the support of many other departments, doctors and nurses could not perform their roles. The whole service, therefore, comprised numerous separate but nonetheless essentially interdependent departments.

From a management viewpoint, the hospital was divided into two main services: administrative and professional, though with regular and essential consultations between the two. General policy and day-to-day running of the hospital was the responsibility of the commanding officer and his senior officers – executive and senior administrative officers, adjutant and chief nurse. Included within the administrative section were:

Headquarters – Where the 'top brass' were based.

Personnel office – Responsible for keeping staff records, and ensuring that staff were paid monthly on time.

Registrar's office – Maintained patients' medical and clinical records from arrival at the hospital, and during their stay, to final discharge. Also dealt with admissions and dispositions of patients.

General Supply – Acquired all supplies other than medical, including procurement and issue of clothing, cleaning materials, motor parts, petrol and oil, and many other items essential for a smooth running hospital. The unit also handled shoe repairs for all ranks and organised laundry and dry-cleaning.

Medical Supply – Acquired and supplied all consumables and equipment needed by doctors and nurses in the surgical and medical departments of the hospital. These included such items as sterile dressings, towels, vomit bowls, transfusion sets, catheters, syringes and needles. The unit also maintained a ready supply of penicillin stored at a constant temperature in refrigerators. It sterilized and disinfected surgical instruments and other items in its autoclaves and sterilizers. Also based in this section, the hospital employed a civilian seamstress whose job was to repair torn linen and any other similar items for the whole hospital.

Pharmacy – Like any hospital today, this department dispensed drugs on prescription for both inpatients and outpatients.

Headquarters building 27 and American flag. (Winston Hawkins)

GH Commanding Officer, Lt. Col. Daniel Sheehan at bottom of steps leading up to US flag. Motor pool is in the background. (Molly Placko)

The records office. (74th GH records – NARA)

Autoclaves. (56th GH records – NARA)

Pharmacy staff of 74th GH. (74th GH records – NARA)

74th GH – pharmacy technician taking penicillin from refrigerator 3 November 1944. (Dr. Sanders Marble)

Chapel – Protestant and Catholic faiths shared the use of the chapel facilities.

Utilities Department – From first arriving at Tyntesfield, this was one of the busiest departments in the hospital. It was responsible for general maintenance work to ensure that all hospital facilities – buildings, water supply, electricity, telephones, waste disposal, etc – functioned properly at all times. In addition to the work previously described, this unit implemented many improvements to enable workers in all departments to perform more efficiently. These included making racks for blank forms in the nurses' offices, footstools and sitting stools for surgeons in the operating suite, splash-boards for ward sluice rooms, and cupboards and shelves to simplify the working of many other departments.

Motor Pool – Without properly maintained road vehicles, the hospital could not function. The men of the motor pool maintained in full working order all essential forms of transport: ambulances and buses for transporting the wounded, lorries for hauling goods from storage depots to the hospital, and personnel cars and Jeeps.

PX (Post Exchange) – The Post Exchange, universally known throughout American forces as the PX, the American equivalent of the British NAAFI, provided an essential service to both patients and hospital staff. It sold most of their personal needs including toiletries, lipsticks and perfume, cigarettes, chocolate bars, peanuts, candies [sweets and confectionery], Wrigley's Juicy Fruit Gum, razor blades, soap, stockings, cigarettes, American canned beers and other drinks, and condoms. Moreover, a ready supply of cigarettes and occasional nylon stockings were available, a sure winner for a GI introducing himself to and flirting with local girls; and chewing gum always delighted local children.

Mailroom, barber's shop and tailor – Mail was one of the chief morale builders to both hospital staff and wounded alike in time of war, so handling it efficiently and distributing it promptly was essential. And soldiers periodically needed a hair trim, and repairs and adjustments to uniforms and other clothing, so the barber and tailor provided these essential services. It is believed that nurses mostly used local civilian hairdressers or talents within their own ranks.

Leisure facilities – Separate clubrooms for officers and nurses, and for other ranks provided facilities in which to relax in off-duty time.

*Chapel at the 19th
General Hospital
Blackmore Park,
Malvern. The chapel
at Tyntesfield was
identical. (19th GH
records – NARA)*

*Main entrance,
spring 1944. (Win-
ston Hawkins)*

*Group of 56th GH enlisted men outside
Post Exchange (PX), building 49.
(Winston Hawkins)*

The Professional Services

The professional services comprised two theoretically separate departments: surgical and medical, though their roles inevitably overlapped at times. As its name implies, the surgical department of the hospital performed surgery on patients whereas the medical side treated conditions generally not requiring surgery, but nonetheless provided wide-ranging medical care. And many other services performed their roles within the hospital, without which the surgical and medical departments could not function. These included:

Roentgenological – More commonly called the X-Ray department, it provided an indispensable service to surgeons tasked with setting broken bones and removing foreign objects from wounded patients. Many patients had sustained bone fractures and muscle damage, and many bodies contained metal fragments. Without X-rays to locate and identify bone fractures, and to localize embedded metal fragments, the surgeon would grope almost blindly. The X-ray (radiology) department, therefore, was always busy.

Laboratory – The laboratory service comprised six major departments: Bacteriology, Chemistry, Serology, Hematology, Pathology, Parasitology. A major with a captain as his second-in-command was responsible for the service, while enlisted technicians carried out the analysis work. A detailed explanation of the roles of each department is beyond the scope of this book; suffice to say, the departments individually and collectively examined samples of vomit,

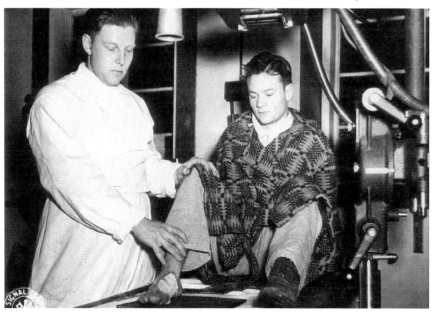

74th GH – technician taking X-ray of soldiers foot 4 November 1944. (Dr. Sanders Marble)

74th GH – labo-ratory technicians conducting blood cell counts 4 November 1944. (Dr. Sanders Marble)

Laboratory. (56th GH records – NARA)

Laboratory. (74th GH records – NARA)

faeces, blood, urine, tissue and many other bodily specimens to assist doctors in diagnosing patients' ills, enabling them to prescribe appropriate medication or other action. Another routine task performed was analysing the mains water to ensure that the supply maintained the high standard required. Organising and selecting prospective blood donors, typing blood and maintaining a list of suitable donors was also within the laboratory service's remit.

Only one death on the post is recorded in the 56th's records. Nonetheless, the morgue was an essential facility. Deaths did occur in nearby camps and on the roads, and post-mortems were carried out at the hospital. Responsibility for supervising and maintaining the morgue also fell to the laboratory service, and its various departments examined body samples to assist in determining cause of death.

Dental – The dental service comprised five officers and eleven sergeants of varying grades. The service operated in a ten-room building with coke stoves heating all the rooms. Records do not say how many chairs were in use, but it does say that one electric drilling engine was used, all others being foot-operated. The CO wryly observed that *by the end of the day, dentists using the foot-operated machines have an aching leg.* This department was continually busy providing dental treatment for both patients and staff of the hospital, and for outpatients from the many units based in the area. In addition to normal routine inspections, fillings and extractions, the service also made, fitted and repaired partial and full dentures to replace missing teeth, and, perhaps oddly for a dental department, artificial eyes (see EENT following).

EENT – This department routinely examined staff's and patients' eyes and prescribed, made and fitted glasses. It also treated patients suffering from injury, disease and other disorders of the eyes, ears, nose and throat.

As the war progressed, the army faced a growing demand for artificial eyes since approximately two per cent of all injuries involved eyes. Men lost eyes in accidents and combat, and, perhaps surprisingly, one-eyed recruits were allowed into the army under lower physical standards. Up to the end of 1943, eyes were made of glass, and these sometimes fell out of sockets and smashed. But, in 1944, Captain Stanley F Erpf, working in the army dental section with the 30th General Hospital at Mansfield, England, started to make artificial eyes from acrylic resin used in making dentures. Unlike the glass eye, the acrylic-resin eye was almost indestructible, and, when properly coloured and painted, matched exactly a patient's good eye, a feature of great psychological benefit. Moreover, they stayed in place better than glass eyes.

Dispensary – This section handled sick call and also gave periodic immunization injections.

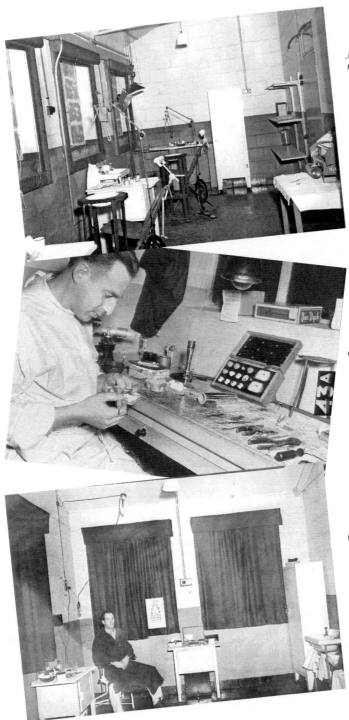

Dental clinic Note foot-operated drilling machines. (56th GH records – NARA)

74th GH – technician preparing mould for an artificial eye 5 November 1944. (Dr. Sanders Marble)

Patient waiting in EENT reception. (56th GH records – NARA)

Operating two hospitals

While running the hospital at Tyntesfield, the parent unit had still to fulfil its role at Malvern Wells, so constant liaison between the two units had to be maintained. Because those assigned to Tyntesfield were classed only as a detachment, no additional staff or vehicles were made available for the unit's dual function. So, in the period when both units were operating, personnel of the parent unit and Detachment A journeyed back and forth to serve interchangeably at both sites. Since transportation between the two locations could be best accomplished only by road, the continual shuttling caused obvious inconvenience, both in loss of usable time for essential personnel and in tying up motor vehicles. Had both units been operating at full capacity instead of at about one-third capacity, the situation might well have been grave.

But, despite the problems associated with operating in two locations, the 56th celebrated its first Christmas in England with a traditional dinner at noon on 25 December 1943. As personnel were caring for patients at both Malvern Wells and Tyntesfield, presumably dinner was served at both locations. However, official records do not tell us. The fare listed on the menu comprised roast turkey, celery, dressing, mashed potatoes, giblet gravy, cranberry sauce, creamed corn, sweet pickles, sliced cheese, minced pie, hot rolls and butter, hot coffee and candy.

Lt Col Sheehan provided his own personal message as a foreword to the menu:

> *Seasons Greetings to all personnel 56th General Hospital*
> *I would like on this occasion to extend to all of you a sincere wish for a merry Christmas and a happy New Year.*
> *Your cooperation and individual effort during the past several months far exceeded my fondest expectations. By persisting in the same high standards, I am confident that the 56th General Hospital will find the New Year bright and hopeful and will contribute a noteworthy chapter in the history of the Medical Department to the winning of this war.*

The division of the 56th into two groups proved to be short-lived, however. From the outset of operations in the UK, the intention had always been that the hospital would operate as a single unit at Tyntesfield. So, effective from midnight 12 January 1944, the 56th handed over its patients at Malvern Wells to the 96th General Hospital and, on 13 January 1944, all personnel transferred to Tyntesfield. There, at one minute past midnight the next day, the hospital officially became the headquarters of the 56th GH, and Detachment A was absorbed into the headquarters unit. On that day also, the status of the 750-bed station hospital was raised to that of a 1,000-bed general hospital in preparation for the invasion of Europe.

When a working routine had become established at Tyntesfield, the overall view of the commanding officer was that the layout of the hospital buildings had been well thought out. The operating suite and surgical wards were well located relative to the site entrance, with surgical and medical wards grouped around the operating suite, X-ray dept, etc. Convalescent wards had been located farther away so convalescing patients needing to return to surgical and X-ray departments were generally taken by ambulance because the inclines within the complex, albeit gentle to a fit person, were formidable to a man using crutches. The motor pool and headquarters buildings were also well located close to the hospital entrance. Mess facilities were well grouped together in the western half of the site. Perhaps the worst located buildings were the nurses' quarters, at the most south-easterly end of the complex, entailing a walk of 1/3 mile or so to get to the surgical wards. The walk would likely have been enjoyed on a fine summer's morning or evening, but loathed in driving rain or snow. Some enterprising nurses, however, soon acquired bicycles to speed up their journeying.

Although with much mostly good-natured grumbling, hospital staff learned to live with the minor inadequacies and irritations, and the spartan toilet and bathing facilities. But the one feature of all buildings throughout the hospital complex that proved to be the most inadequate and caused most grumbles among the personnel was the form of heating.

View along internal lower road towards Motor Pool. Building 26 middle right. (Molly Placko)

View towards hospital entrance from adjacent to building 29 (not in photograph) at left. (Molly Placko)

In his report, Lt Col Sheehan recorded:

To keep these stoves supplied with fuel, stoked and policed, was undoubtedly one of the largest single drains on manpower in the unit.

[The term 'policed' probably derives from US military usage where the word is used as a verb to 'keep in order'.]

Nonetheless, despite the grumbles, Lt Col Sheehan favourably reported:

In an overall estimate of the entire hospital in regard to buildings and accommodation, it can be said that the organization considered itself most fortunate in its assignment to the site.

Shortly after Detachment A opened the hospital, it took on civilian workers in various roles to release enlisted men for other duties. As at 1 April 1944, the hospital employed seventeen civilians full-time: two typists, three telephone operators, five cleaners, four gardeners, one electrician, one carpenter and one seamstress. It also employed ten civilians working part-time: nine cleaners and one carpenter. Although not part of the hospital function, one building was made available to the British *Deputy Comander Royal Engineers* (DCRE) that employed ten full-time and thirteen part-time civilians. The DCRE role was to oversee construction of the many camps for American and British military units in its area of jurisdiction, and a permanent base within the hospital grounds was ideally situated.

Main entrance showing motor pool, winter 1943/spring 1944. (56th GH records – NARA)

Two soldiers of 56th GH at main entrance April/May 1944. (Winston Hawkins)

View along internal lower road towards Motor Pool. Shadow of building 27b at bottom left corner. (56th GH records – NARA)

In his report covering the period from 18 October 1943 to 1 April 1944, Lt Col Sheehan recorded:

> *...cleaners and maintenance people carried out their duties satisfactorily, but in the more skilled jobs – clerical, typists, telephone operators, etc – the performance of the civilians was not so good. It took longer to train British workers in these roles, than American enlisted men, and the Americans were 'more efficient, conscientious and reliable operators' than civilians.*

The work of a Station Hospital

In November 1943, when the first member of the 56th GH arrived at Tyntesfield, battle casualties in United States forces in the UK were almost exclusively confined to Air Force air and ground crews, their bases being mainly in the counties of Norfolk, Suffolk, Northamptonshire and Bedfordshire. In the main, hospitals near to the air bases dealt with these casualties. Consequently, Tyntesfield handled almost no battle casualties. However, the large number of troop concentrations nearby provided the 56th with a steady flow of patients requiring its services, particularly the outpatient and dispensary departments.

The hospital was fully equipped to deal with most medical and surgical conditions, and could provide all the services found in today's hospitals for outpatients and for inpatients requiring surgery or prolonged assessment of their condition. As in medical centres in any village or town today, doctors and nurses of the 56th dealt with an assortment of conditions, most similar to those found in peacetime: the common cold, influenza, headaches, stomach pains, measles and mumps, neuro-psychiatric disorders, and many other miscellaneous ills. And, in addition, the staff dealt with many military-related ailments: sore feet, legs and ankles from marching in ill-fitting boots or on hard roads, accidents using military equipment and firearms, and the inevitable bloody nose from fist fights. But, whatever the cause of pain or discomfort, the medical staff dealt with them all. In many cases, all that a patient required was a friendly pat on the head and a reassuring smile. Others received a gruff rebuke for wasting time; some were directed to the pharmacy and sent on their way with a handful of pills, while others were admitted as inpatients for more extensive investigation of their complaint.

The orthopaedic department was always very busy dealing with civilian-type orthopaedic injuries including fractures, dislocations and sprains, arthritis, many other bone-related conditions, and the occasional amputation. The dentistry department always had a waiting list; and the X-ray department also rarely had a moment to spare.

The climate and often poorly heated and ventilated living quarters, particularly in tented accommodation, produced a high incidence of mild illness, especially in winter. Diarrhoea and dysentery occasionally broke out, largely attributable to food being stored for too long in the tented camps without adequate refrigeration. Influenza and other respiratory infections accounted regularly for about thirty per cent of all disease among troops. In the winter of 1943/44, an influenza epidemic considerably increased the workload of the doctors and nurses. And, in early 1944, when the 56th was establishing itself, UK troops who had served in North Africa brought back hepatitis and malaria with them.

New units of American soldiers regularly arrived in the UK, often with medical conditions that required surgical attention within days of arriving. These included rectal conditions worsened by constipation on the voyage from the US, hernias and many miscellaneous conditions. Numerous conditions had unknowingly been passed on to troops in the US ports-of-embarkation holding camps. And, additionally, some soldiers entered the UK carrying many contagious diseases including meningitis, chickenpox, tuberculosis, measles and whooping cough.

When the hospital was constructed, a ten-bed isolation ward was allocated for patients with contagious diseases, but this proved to be inadequate. Consequently, a spare main ward was assigned for contagious diseases and individual isolation rooms created by building block partitioning. The original contagious diseases ward was reassigned as a ward for female patients.

The extent of mechanised equipment used by the US Army in WWII accounted for many non-combat injuries; some resulting from unavoidable accidents, but often from lack of care in using potentially dangerous equipment. And road traffic accidents also accounted for a high intake of soldiers requiring anything from patching up to major surgery. The bicycle was a form of transport not commonly used by the American soldier at home. In fact, some GIs had never ridden a bicycle before coming to the United Kingdom. But, in the UK, with its many villages having no or infrequent public transport, and private motor vehicles not readily available due to petrol shortage, the Americans soon realised that a bicycle for local journeying was almost a necessity. Local people brought ancient bicycles out of retirement to sell to the American servicemen and women. Although in 1940 a second-hand bicycle would normally sell for £2 to £3, the price amazingly inflated after the Americans arrived, £10 to £20 being not uncommon. Despite this clear exploitation by the astute 'locals', American servicemen and women willingly paid the asking price.

Many GIs, however, regretted their decision to rest their feet and take to the bicycle. Unfamiliar with riding on the left side of the road, unable to spot lurking hazards in the blackout, occasionally possessing a befuddled brain after an evening in the local pub downing strange alcoholic beverages, he, and sometimes she, often ended their journey sprawled in the road or roadside ditch nursing a fractured wrist, arm or leg. In many American units around the UK, and probably at Tyntesfield too, the bicycle was often referred to as 'Hitler's Secret Weapon'.

But road accidents were not restricted to riders of bicycles. Estimates suggest that, by the end of March 1944, 104,000 American vehicles regularly used British roads, the most common of these being Jeeps and 2½-ton trucks. In the period from July 1942 through March 1944, nearly 29,000 accidents occurred in the UK involving American vehicles, 372 being fatal. But well over 24,000 of them occurred after July 1943. Contrary to the image of the fast-driving Yank, only about one-sixth of these were the result of speeding, and then usually in the blackout at night. More commonly, GI drivers failed to cope with the narrow lanes and general lack of space on UK roads. Side-swiping caused roughly one-third of accidents as drivers on the left side of the vehicle – over ninety-five per cent of American vehicles used in the UK were left-hand drive – tried to pass or overtake on the narrow roads. And a quarter of accidents occurred at speeds less than 5 mph, often as drivers of large trucks reversed or parked. Not all accidents resulted in injury, however, but no doubt the medical staff of the 56th had their fair share of patching up road accident victims.

Injuries to Jeep drivers and passengers accounted for an abnormal number of traffic victims requiring the attentions of army doctors and surgeons. Made by Willys and the Ford Motor Company in America, the Jeep was officially known as the ¼-ton 4x4 General Purpose or GP truck – hence the derived name Jeep – and was the most versatile and commonly used of all army vehicles. The GIs boasted that the Jeep could '...do anything a horse could do except eat oats'. Its open cockpit and no seat belts provided practically no protection for the driver and passengers. It was constructed like an old-fashioned horse-drawn wagon, with hard suspension, so that people riding in it were often thrown out when travelling over rough ground or bumpy roads at even moderate speeds. The vehicle possessed peculiar characteristics that most commonly caused hip dislocation or fracture to those thrown from it. Its seats were so low that the rider's hips were flexed more acutely than in other vehicles, and the posture of the rider did not always adjust while travelling through the air before hitting the ground. The combination of the Jeep's peculiar characteristics and the excitement and recklessness of men at war, most of whom were young, produced a high incidence of serious injury from accidents. In a survey of severe injury caused to Jeep riders, all but one, a fifty-one year-old, were to men aged between nineteen and thirty-three years, the period of life in which trauma always exacts its greatest toll.

The need for routines

The Americans recognised that a prerequisite of a well-run military hospital was that every person involved knew precisely what to do without having to think about their role, particularly when receiving many casualties in a short time period. Therefore, standardising procedures and developing a good working relationship between doctors, nurses and medically trained, enlisted men was essential. During their time at Tyntesfield, the 56th medical staff developed this confidence by carrying out so-called 'elective surgery'. Elective surgery included operations on hammertoes, on the spine – particularly for prolapsed discs – on shoulders, on knee joints, and for hernias, varicose veins and appendicitis. This type of work accounted for the largest number of procedures performed by the surgeons of the 56th while at Tyntesfield. Some of this surgery was clearly essential, but in many cases a surgeon advised his patient that surgery was desirable rather than essential, the aim always being to return the soldier to combat fitness.

If, however, the advice of World War I surgeons had been heeded, a great many elective operations, particularly on the feet and the knee joints, would never have been performed in World War II. Alas, this good advice was generally ignored and many of the operations were often unnecessarily intrusive – micro-surgery had yet to be thought of – and they usually failed to achieve their objective which was to increase the number of combat soldiers. Eventually, after a great deal of time and effort had been wasted, it was realized that most of these operations were, for all practical purposes, complete failures. It was the exception rather than the rule for a soldier to be able to resume a full combat role after any elective operation, and often he could do no more after the operation than before. Some of this misplaced surgical enthusiasm could be attributed to the scarcity of work available to surgeons in the period before D-Day but, post war, it was argued that most of it could be explained by a lack of mature judgment by US Army surgeons. It was also acknowledged that some elective surgery was performed on soldiers whose deformities were so severe and of such long standing that they should never have been sent to a combat zone in the first place.

But, by D-Day, the problem practically solved itself. The demands on the surgeons' time to treat combat injuries was such that soldiers genuinely requiring elective surgery were invariably returned to hospitals in America, and few of those ever returned to Europe in a combat role.

In the period from 1 January 1944 to 9 May 1944, the hospital performed 933 elective surgery operations.

Treatment of civilians and British soldiers

Despite the large concentration of American troops in the area covered by the 56th during its time at Tyntesfied, the 834 beds were never all occupied at any one time. In fact, the peak bed occupancy was 582 on 29 February 1944. Shortly after the hospital opened on 15 November 1943, American authorities allocated fifty beds to civilians requiring surgery to help relieve the acute hospitalisation problems within the local health service, and, for the most part, male patients occupied these beds.

One civilian who benefited from the facilities offered by the Americans was Peter Abbey. In late 1943/early 1944, Peter worked for BOAC [British Overseas Airways Corporation] as a transport officer. While helping to load an aircraft at Bristol's Whitchurch Airport, he suffered a hernia, necessitating an operation to repair the injury. At that time, the Bristol hospital authorities were severely overstretched, so his doctor and the Bristol Royal Infirmary arranged for the operation to be performed by an American doctor at the 56th General Hospital. Peter recalls:

Captain Ravitch carried out the operation; and 1st Lt Lois Halpin from South Dakota, a nurse in the hospital looked after me during my recovery period. I was initially given a local anaesthetic (epidural) in my spine, but the effects soon wore off so I was then given Sodium Pentothal as a general anaesthetic.

*I was in the hospital for at least two weeks sometime at the start of 1944 and received three letters. The postmarks on the letters were dated 19 Jan, 24 Jan and 1 Feb 1944, so I was obviously in at that time. I also had a visit from my then girlfriend, a Chief Petty Officer in the Wrens [officially **WRNS** – Women's Royal Naval Service – popularly known as the Wrens].*

The food in the hospital was good, given the wartime general shortage. I remember having tinned pineapple in with a salad with raw cabbage. Fresh eggs were difficult to come by, and powdered egg brought over from America was the norm. My sister visited me in hospital and brought some fresh eggs from a friend's farm at Clutton, south of Bristol. She gave some to the Americans and as thanks, they gave me something like 4000 cigarettes in packs of 200. My sister brought in an old suitcase in which to take them all home, and it took me months to smoke them! I remember the main cigarette brands as Beechnut, Herbert Tarrington, Chesterfield and Lucky Strike.

When I was able to walk around, I was given an American red dressing gown made from a corduroy type material, with MDUSA in silver thread embroidered on the top left breast area. It stood for Medical Department United States Army, but the Americans ghoulishly quipped that it stood for Many Die You (U) Shall Also! During my convalescing period, I was taken from the ward in a Jeep to the recreation hall [building 34] where there was some entertainment, but I can't remember any details.

The kindness and interest shown by doctors and all members of the staff was outstanding.

Captain Ravitch, a doctor who trained at the John Hopkins Hospital in Baltimore before the war, went on to become one of America's leading hernia specialists after returning to America.

A nurse, who spent some time in the civilian ward, recalled the peculiarly British ritual for drinking tea:

> *We learned to make British-style tea. This was drunk before breakfast, at 10:00 am, 2:00 pm, and at night.*

At the beginning of April 1944 taking the war directly to the enemy on land was clearly imminent, so the facility for treating civilians was withdrawn. By 1 April 1944, the hospital had treated 156 civilian patients, a huge contribution towards relieving the burden on the local health service.

The war remained distant for the doctors and nursing staff at Tyntesfield, and traumatic surgery remained surprisingly rare. However, in the latter weeks of February, the hospital started to receive casualties from the Mediterranean theatre of fighting. These casualties, mostly soldiers of the British Army from North Africa had arrived at Bristol's Avonmouth docks in British hospital ships. Most had suffered severe injuries, some of them many months earlier. They had been treated in hospitals in the area where they were wounded, but not always well, and were returned to the UK for further treatment. Some of them were very ill and undernourished when admitted.

Among this group of patients were many interesting medical cases not seen by American doctors before. These included hepatitis, malaria, diphtheria and its complications, and several tropical diseases seldom seen by doctors outside tropical countries. The 56th's doctors assessed these patients' injuries and medical needs and many were transferred to other hospitals for more specialised treatment. However, a few of the more seriously wounded remained at Tyntesfield for a considerable length of time and showed gratifying improvement, such that, by the time of discharge, most had gained an average ten pounds in weight.

Overall, the British soldiers who ended up at Tyntesfield greatly appreciated the treatment and consideration they received from the American doctors, nurses and surgical and medical technicians, and many wrote letters to the American authorities expressing their thanks. However, some grumbled about being served their last meal of the day at five o'clock in the late afternoon, and they did not like some American foods.

Although most of the surgical staff had studied the elements of battle-wound management and care, the arrival of British soldiers was their first opportunity to directly treat battle casualties. Despite their satisfaction at obtaining 'hands-on' experience, they were, nonetheless, left with a feeling of discontent. In his annual report for 1944, Lt Col Sheehan, recorded:

Unfortunately, we came at once into abrupt contact with the factor in war surgery most discouraging to the clinician – the rapid and sudden evacuation of patients, precluding any hope of observation of any but the immediate results of therapy. Nevertheless, we all felt closer to the war and began to feel we had some more intimate knowledge of what awaited us.

Lt Col Sheehan, like many American senior officers, was keen to cement inter-allied relationships. He demonstrated a thoughtful sensitivity towards British patients in his care and welcomed the numerous British family members who came to the hospital to visit their wounded relatives. On their behalf, the British Red Cross, liaising with their American counterparts, made arrangements with families in the local community to provide overnight accommodation for relatives of wounded British soldiers so that they could be near to them.

Training continues

All doctors, nurses, non-commissioned officers, technicians and other enlisted men had attended medical or training school in the United States and learned the theory about their particular discipline. Although a necessary part of training, learning from books and classroom demonstrations and exercises didn't compare with hands-on experience so great emphasis was placed on informal instruction throughout the administrative departments, in the wards, in the operating rooms and in the clinics of the hospital.

Hawley pointed out:

Few physicians ever see in civil practice injuries of the type that occur in war. They do not know how to care for such injuries properly and unless given special training they will care for them improperly.

So, Hawley insisted that his doctors, nurses and enlisted men remedy this deficiency in their medical knowledge. Therefore, during late winter and early spring 1943/44, with its relatively light patient load, the 56th's medical personnel attended courses at various training centres in American and British hospitals throughout the UK where they had the opportunity of observing actual operations on real casualties, mostly from the Mediterranean area conflicts. American doctors and medical staff also learned much from British doctors in treating burns victims and in plastic surgery techniques, an expertise developed by British doctors over three years of air warfare. They also studied all the latest information about the properties and effects of new drugs, particularly the new wonder drug penicillin which started to be available to all general hospitals in the UK by the end of December 1943.

Also, during February 1944, the 56th's hospital personnel carried out training exercises in evacuating 300 battle casualties, including 150 litter cases, from Tyntesfield to a hospital train at Bristol Temple Meads station, and from the hospital train back to the hospital. The exercise covered all phases including records processing, baggage handling, and restocking the train with essential items. In addition to these exercises, some 56th GH personnel gained experience in handling actual battle casualties in large numbers when they assisted in unloading hospital ships at Bristol's Avonmouth docks, where casualties from the Mediterranean theatre continued to return to England for further care. These casualties, however, most probably went to the 298th General Hospital at Frenchay, north of Bristol, and none to the 56th.

Supplies

Tyntesfield was fortunate in being located only about seven miles from America's largest general supply depot in the UK – G-35 at Bristol – which stocked food and general and medical supplies. In the main, medical supplies were readily available but many incidental items, trivial in some regards but so vital to the smooth running of a hospital, were not always obtainable. All departments learned to improvise and conserve essential items of equipment. In her war's-end summary, the chief nurse reported:

> *It was here that we really learned to conserve materials and improvise equipment. Gauze was washed, rinsed and reused; all small Dreene [trade name] shampoo bottles were saved and used for narcotic tablets; paper clips and bobby pins served as tubing clamps; thermometer cases were used as sterile containers for needles; drinking tubes of plastic tubing were most satisfactory; a glass connector inside a piece of rubber tubing and inserted into a hole in the bottom of a plasma can was ideal for irrigation. The nurses assumed the attitude best described by that old motto 'I'll find a way or make one'.*
>
> *We spent a lot of time making equipment for surgery. Drapes, sick pads, masks, cutting and folding gauze, washing beds, making beds, sorting equipment, standardising cupboards, wards and bedside tables. There is not a nurse overseas who does not hate the word standardise, but it does make for a neater, better organised, smoother operating unit. We also ran into difficulty classifying some of the British material we had to use. For weeks we used the small gay-coloured squares sent to us for bedside tables, until we discovered that they were the English version of bed-pan covers.*

The approach of D-Day

At the turn of the year into 1944, although the date of the invasion of mainland Europe was yet to be decided, most with any military connections reasoned that it would take place in the summer of that year. By April 1944, thousands of GIs had progressively moved from their training bases to assemble in marshalling areas in the counties of Hampshire, Dorset, Devon and Cornwall near to south coast ports from where the American element of the sea-borne invasion would be launched. These troops required continuing medical facilities and feeding, so, from about the middle of April, small specialist teams were detached from American hospitals and sent to the marshalling areas. The medical teams provided last-minute attention to ailments and injuries suffered by the soldiers, and also weeded out those with more serious conditions or disabilities and transferred them to hospitals where proper treatment could be given.

Consequently, a team of thirty men comprising dental, medical and mess officers, enlisted technical assistants and cooks, on detachment from the 56th, transferred to camps in the marshalling areas. The severest handicap to the 56th was the loss of twenty-one cooks and mess staff out of their total complement of thirty-three. However, they coped by increasing the working hours of those remaining and assigning other personnel to mess duties to fill the breach. Additionally, a number of clerks and truck drivers were also detached from the 56th for duties at the marshalling areas.

On 23 April 1944, Lt Col Sheehan received orders confirming that the 56th would be one of the hospital units to transfer to France about six weeks after the invasion. Its role would be to provide forward surgical and medical facilities near to the front line. Providing medical care near to the front line in temporary (tented) accommodation, possibly under enemy fire, would be a totally different experience. Consequently, the unit was ordered to relocate to Hoylake, a town situated on the Wirral peninsula between the Rivers Mersey and Dee and approximately eight miles from Liverpool. Here, all personnel would undergo specialised training for the unfamiliar operating conditions they would encounter in France, and wherever else they might be assigned. So, in three separate parties, on 8, 11 and 14 May 1944, the unit's personnel and equipment left Tyntesfield by rail and road and headed for Hoylake. The last to leave were administration staff, whose final act was to hand over the plant to the 74th General Hospital.

Statistics Summary

The following summary covers the period that the 56th operated at Tyntesfield; that is, from 15 November 1943 to 8 May 1944:

Admissions

From units and dispensaries	3,462
By transfer from other hospitals[1]	583
Highest census (29 February 1944)	582
Lowest census not applicable, it was zero when the hospital opened	

[1] Includes 243 from Det 'A' to main unit

Dispositions

Returned to duty	2,713
Patients transferred to other hospitals[2]	960
Patients returned to the United States	165

[2] Includes 416 from 56th GH to 74th GH which took over from them.

Outpatients & Dispensary

Visits	5,129
Treatments	7,621
Doctors also made 'sick calls' to units within its catchment.	

Dental

Examinations	2,878
Chair sittings	9,951
Treatments	3,071
Dentures fitted (full & partial from 1/1/44 to 8/5/44)	203

Chapter Five

The 74th General Hospital

The 74th GH is born

The 74th GH was activated on 31 August 1942 at Camp Atterbury, Indiana. Its stated mission, when eventually assigned, would be to 'provide definitive surgical and medical care for patients transferred from hospitals near to the war zone, and for patients from units stationed in the vicinity of the hospital'.

The initial postings to the 74th comprised one medical officer, a number of administrative personnel from Ft McClellen, Alabama, and a group of hospital technicians from Billings General Hospital at Fort Benjamin Harrison, Indiana. Col Hyman I Teperson assumed command of the unit on 17 September 1942.

On 31 October 1942, the unit, now comprising two officers and sixty-two enlisted men transferred to New Orleans, a Port of Embarkation (POE). All medical personnel were assigned for training in the army station hospital operating there. Other enlisted personnel, including medical, surgical, laboratory and X-ray technicians, attended army schools for specialist training. Likewise, men who were to work in other departments, for example, transportation, administration, utilities and mess, also attended appropriate training schools.

74th GH Insignia. (74th GH records – NARA)

On 1 April 1943, the unit moved to Fort Jackson, South Carolina, where training continued in preparation for the day when the 74th would be called upon to undertake its assignment. At this posting, personnel numbers gradually built, including the arrival of approximately one hundred nurses.

While at Fort Jackson, on 22 April 1943, the unit was authorized a distinctive insignia described thus: 'Upon and over a gold sunburst (natural colours) issuant from a maroon scroll with the motto "Health through science" in gold letters, a silver X-ray tube entwined with a maroon serpent'. The maroon and white were the colours of the medical department, also represented by a serpent taken from the staff of Aesculapius, the first Greek mythological God of medicine. The sunburst denoted the oldest

74th GH enlisted men's lapel pin. (Author's collection)

and most permanent of the techniques of healing and therapy, and the X-ray tube represented the newer concept of atomic structure and radioactivity.

Still in training in early February 1944, the unit received advance orders to prepare for a further move, this time to Camp Kilmer. Constructed in 1942, Camp Kilmer lay two miles north of New Brunswick in New Jersey State on the west side of the Hudson River, and approximately twenty-two miles south-west of New York City. The camp was named after Alfred Joyce Kilmer, an American poet and resident of New Brunswick who was killed in 1918 aged thirty-one in the Second Battle of the Marne in France. The location of the camp had been chosen by the United States War Department as the most suitable final staging area for the New York Port of Embarkation. The embarkation piers of New York could easily be reached from the camp by a train journey on the Pennsylvania Railroad to the west side of the Hudson, thence by ferry across the river.

Now fully staffed, on 16 February 1944, the unit departed their Fort Jackson base and boarded the train for Camp Kilmer to ready itself for overseas deployment. At Camp Kilmer, hospital staff attended numerous lectures; sent personal effects home and wrote final letters to family and friends (strictly censored); and received medical injections, new uniforms and other clothing, mess equipment and all the other personal items needed for their forthcoming operations. Security was rigorously enforced: none of the hospital personnel were told where they were going, or the name of the ship in which they would travel. All they knew was that they would soon be off to war.

For nearly two weeks, with little to do in their leisure time, and with hardly any contact with the outside world apart from rare trips into New York, they waited in nervous expectation for something to happen. Then, quite suddenly, Col Teperson received orders that no one was to leave the camp, receive visitors or make telephone calls. Departure could be expected within twenty-four hours.

Eventually, on the dark evening of 29 February 1944, the unit left Camp Kilmer for the nearby railway station and boarded the train that would take them to Weehawken ferry terminal. From there, harbour boats ferried them across the river to a waiting troopship tied up at pier 90. As they arrived at the pier buildings, they looked up at the awesome massive bulk of the ship towering above them that would take them off to war: the *RMS Queen Mary*. At 2:00 am on 1 March, the waiting crowd of servicemen and women began boarding the *Queen* to search out their allocated quarters.

This majestic peacetime cruise-liner, owned by the Cunard Line Limited, had been stripped of all her luxurious fittings and furnishings, and her ten decks fitted out for transporting troops. The ship was close to 1,100 feet long – the length of three football pitches – 118 feet wide, and of 81,000 gross tonnage. Her peacetime livery, predominantly of black and red, had been painted over with a dull 'light sea grey', earning her the nickname *Grey Ghost*. As a luxury peacetime liner, the *Queen* provided accommodation for approximately 2,100 passengers and a crew of 1,100. In her wartime role she would at times carry up to 15,000 troops and their baggage.

RMS Queen Mary that brought the 74th GH to England on Hudson River with the Empire State Building in background.

Destination unknown

Eventually, at noon on 1 March 1944, the mighty ship let go her mooring lines and, at the top of the tide, eased out into the icy waters of the Hudson River. A high-tide sailing was essential to ensure that the keel of the overloaded liner safely cleared the top of the Holland Tunnel that provided a road link between Manhattan Island and Jersey City on the west side of the river. About three miles downstream from her berth, the *Queen* passed over the tunnel, continued south past Liberty Island and headed towards the grey waters of the North Atlantic Ocean and, to most on board, the 'destination unknown'.

On this trip, the *Queen* carried 11,950 mixed Army, Navy and Air Force personnel of which approximately 660 made up the 74th General Hospital's complement, together with the ship's crew numbering 1,190 men. No doubt many of those standing on the upper decks or peering through portholes would have looked back at the receding Liberty Island and its prominent Statute of Liberty, the famous lady with her torch symbolically held aloft, and wondered when, or even whether, they would see her again.

Clear of the Hudson River and in open water, the *Queen* headed east, gradually increasing her speed to cruise at about twenty-eight knots. She travelled unescorted, relying on her speed and zigzagging course changes every seven minutes or so to outmanoeuvre any German U-boats that might still be lurking in the Atlantic. Three days after leaving New York, all on board were told that they were heading for England and the European Theatre of Operations (ETO). Five and a half days after leaving New York, on 7 March 1944, the *Queen* eased her way up Scotland's River Clyde and dropped anchor in Gourock Bay, downstream from the city of Glasgow. She had completed her 3,540-mile crossing averaging nearly twenty-seven knots.

In his report covering the 74th GH's activities in 1944, Col Teperson, its commanding officer, simply observed that the Atlantic crossing was 'uneventful'. But those on board later described the crossing as anything but a pleasure cruise. Officers were assigned to cabins in which bunks had been constructed for about twenty men and women – all female nurses held officer rank – in what were formally four-berth cabins. By comparison, enlisted men roughed it. Bunks and hammocks had been crammed into every available space, mostly on lower decks, but also in upper-deck staterooms and some corridors, with only eighteen inches between stacked bunks. In the former first-class section, twelve bunks occupied the same space as one bed in peacetime. Enlisted men double bunked: half of them spent twenty-four hours sleeping on the decks with a couple of blankets for warmth while the other half spent the same time in the bunks; then the next night they swapped around.

The former first-class dining room had been converted into the main mess hall, accommodating 2,000 men at a single sitting. But the food generally was poor compared with what Americans were used to: kidney stew or boiled mutton, and Brussels sprouts and bitter marmalade were typically standard fare. Two meals were served daily: breakfast from 6:30 to 11:00 am, and supper from 3:00 to 7:30 pm. Enlisted men spent a large part of their time queuing in line waiting to eat, but many of them were so disgusted with the food that they preferred standing in other endless lines at the PXs to buy 'snacking' food to supplement their diet. Officers ate in the former tourist-class lounge dining on regular tables and served by enlisted men acting as stewards.

All facilities provided on the *Queen* had been designed for approximately 3,300 individuals only. One major inconvenience experienced by all was the general shortage of on-board water. As a troopship, the ship's water supply had to meet the needs of five times the number it had been designed for, so regular washing and showering, a fastidious obsession with many Americans, had to take second place to providing drinking water. Another major problem was that toilet facilities were inadequate, and queuing for over an hour to use the toilet was not uncommon. And to add to their concerns, if the ship had to be hurriedly evacuated at sea, those souls crammed into the lower decks would have had little chance of escape. Had they succeeded, the number of lifeboats and rafts was inadequate for the numbers on board.

James (Jim) Carter, a Medical Technician Fifth Grade (T/5), recalled after the war:

> *The crossing on the Queen Mary was rough with quite a bit of seasickness. It was said that the ship changed course every 7 min to avoid German submarines. We dropped anchor off Gourock, Scotland. I remember the pretty little village at 7am in the dawn. We left the Queen Mary by boat to Gourock.*

And Alice Boehret, a twenty-five year-old second lieutenant nurse with the 74th, recalls her recollections of the journey:

> *Well, I got seasick, and I really got seasick! So I took Seconal, and evidently I'm allergic to it, because I broke out with rheumatic erythema. So when we got to Glasgow, I had to be taken off the boat with another nurse and several men who were sick and taken to a hospital outside Glasgow, American hospital, and I was there for several weeks. Then I was shipped alone by train, strange money in my pocket, to Liverpool.*

Left: *Alvy DeHart & Jim Carter (right) of the 74th GH at Tyntesfield. (Jim Carter via Nailsea & District Local History Society)*

Below left: *Joe Coughlin and Jim Carter (right) of the 74th GH. (Jim Carter via Nailsea & District Local History Society)*

Above: *74th GH nurse 2nd Lt. Alice Boehret – 1944. (University of North Carolina)*

Left: *74th GH nurse Alice Boehret's cabin card on Queen Mary. (University of North Carolina)*

BOEHRET, ALICE C.   2nd Lt.

NAME & RANK

Queen Mary 1- March 1944

ROOM M-57

KEEP THIS CARD

England – staging area at Hoylake

The day after arriving in Scotland, the 74th General Hospital's personnel disembarked onto lighters and ferries that transferred them to the Scottish mainland. At Gourock station, they boarded trains that would take them to their next staging post at Hoylake, Cheshire, on the Wirrall peninsula, although at time of boarding this was yet another 'destination unknown'.

Jim Carter further recalls:

> The train stopped at Carlisle where the Red Cross, I believe, treated us with refreshments. A little group of men, wearing colorful kilts, were playing bagpipes for us. On our journey how well I remember the women waving to us from their back gardens as they hung out their wash. That greeting meant a lot to us. The date was March 8, 1944. Our unit didn't have a clue about our final destination. Our next stop was Hoylake (West Kirby) at 9 pm and we marched into this town with dogs barking at us strangers invading their town at night. We were billeted in the vacant neighborhood houses.

All nurses were billeted with local families in their homes, as were some of the enlisted men. The rest of the enlisted men were sent to eight houses, and the officers to others, all houses having beforehand been requisitioned by the unit's billeting officer cooperating with local authorities. Most of the requisitioned houses had been used by British troops for similar purposes during the preceding four years and were generally in poor condition. Mostly, they were dirty, with soiled woodwork and floors, dirty and often non-functional toilet equipment, and with occasional blocked drains.

The unit's commanding officer's report to the American authorities covering the period from 8 to 31 March 1944 states:

> The situation was complicated by the fact that neither the British liaison officer nor our quartermaster depot provided a supply of mops, brooms, lye, soap or other cleaning equipment or materials in sufficient quantity to make conditions liveable for the personnel housed. These items of equipment were finally procured with private funds of officers placed in charge of each billet and of the men living in them. Improvisation of clothes and equipment hangers, continued attack on dirt and disorder, and repairs by British civilian workmen resulted in great improvement in the condition of these living quarters.

Hot water was available for bathing in only one of the ten requisitioned properties occupied by some of the officers. All other officers and enlisted men had to visit the local municipal baths to get a hot shower, and this was only once a week. For shaving, enlisted men boiled water in kettles on open fire grates, but the officers fared slightly better: they were supplied with electric kettles or small boilers.

Jim Carter again:

> *The house where I stayed was No 4 Queens St. The front room had 4 bunk beds with straw mattresses. I remember so well the hospitality of the people in Hoylake and the welcome. The seafront showers could only accommodate so many men, and people allowed the GIs to use their bathtubs on a scheduled time. Never will I forget that gesture. Marching on the sands and breathing the invigorating air out of the Irish Sea made us hungry all the time.*

By comparison, nurses were quartered in relative luxury with families in their own houses. But even this situation caused some minor difficulties. Many of the nurses, only twenty-one years old, often younger than the daughters of some of the families, were at times treated too protectively and overwhelmed with kindness. Aware that many restrictions were in force in England – food and clothing rationing, bathing water and many others – they were sometimes embarrassed by the kindness shown to them. In a letter home, Alice Boehret commented on the shortage of straightforward everyday items:

> *If you could see the way they save paper over here you would pop! If you buy a cake or a bun at the bake shop they may have a paper bag or they might just hand it to you. Sometimes they wrap it in a piece of newspaper.*

The British early March weather was somewhat colder than that to which many Americans were accustomed. Also, poor heating in most of the requisitioned houses and no heating at all in bedrooms and bathrooms, together with inadequate bedding until army bedrolls arrived, were blamed for the prevailing colds and bronchial problems. Consequently, the numbers reporting sick for almost all of March was high. But, towards the end of the month, the numbers reduced noticeably, so clearly the Americans were becoming acclimatised to the British weather and austere living conditions.

In a letter written on 27 March 1944 to her older sister Dorothy, Alice Boehret said:

> *The country is very beautiful. They say that it is warm here now but I can still see my breath in a room and to me that is <u>cold</u>! I doubt very much if my feet will ever get warm again. You would really be frozen. Yesterday*

I took a bath and could see my breath hang in the air as I breathed. The water was very hot so I didn't mind it. I really do miss ice cream and candy. Never thought that I would especially so soon. Maybe as time passes I'll want it less. I certainly hope so.

I have met some really wonderful people. The ones I am staying with [Mr & Mrs Stevenson] are grand to me. They are wealthy but not snobs in a sense, in another they are very much. We went to tea with them in town on Saturday and had the best pastry I have had in months. And we got extra just because they knew someone.

And the Stevensons thought well of Alice. Mrs Stevenson wrote to Alice's mother in June 1944:

Just to say how much I had enjoyed having her delightful company while she was stationed here. She is a grand girl and we loved her about the house. She was always cheery in spite of worrying a bit about home. She fought her homesickness bravely and did her job well. We, my husband and I, got very fond of her and I hope she will always look upon us as friends…

The unit spent four weeks in training and attending lectures and talks at Hoylake. The local municipal authorities provided speakers to talk on such subjects as local history, geography, Shakespeare and local bird life. Speakers enlightened them about British customs and conditions, the British currency, on general military and medical subjects, and many other incidental issues; and, most importantly, on treating combat injuries, unfamiliar to most American doctors, nurses and enlisted men in the surgical section of the unit. And there was the inevitable physical training, marching, saluting and preparing all in the unit to perform the retreat parade held every Friday afternoon. Before joining the unit, some hospital personnel, nurses in particular, had little or no experience of military procedures.

Commanding Officer of 74th GH, Col. Hyman Teperson. (University of Tennessee)

To Tyntesfield

On 8 May 1944, Colonel Teperson received orders to transfer the unit to Tyntesfield to operate US Army Hospital Plant no 4165 in the county of Somerset and to relieve and replace the 56th General Hospital under the command of Lieutenant Colonel Daniel Sheehan. The next day, the 74th GH's personnel packed up their belongings and boarded trains for yet another 'destination unknown'.

Jim Carter again:

> *We left Hoylake on May 8 [9th?] 1944 and started our journey to Bristol. The train pulled into Temple Meads Station and we were trucked to a place called Tyntesfield close to Nailsea. There the 74th Gen'l Hospital made its headquarters and we lived in barracks and worked the hospital wards.*

Formal transfer of the hospital and its 437 resident patients, from the 56th to the 74th, took place on 10 May 1944. Colonel Teperson reported that he considered the 74th fortunate in taking over a hospital wherein most facilities had been well established by its predecessor. Although the 56th had carried out many improvements at the post, including building a covered walkway to link the operating suite to the surgical wards, and adding some purpose-made ward equipment and furniture, the utilities department of the new occupants immediately embarked upon further projects to improve the lot of all and enable the hospital to run more efficiently. They built additional covered walkways to link other wards, and a transverse covered walkway to link the medical area of the site to the remote nurses' quarters. In all, they built 3,530 feet of covered walkways. They also greatly improved roads within the hospital, particularly in the area of the operating suite and surgical wards to facilitate ambulance loading and unloading.

74th GH mascot – note he is wearing glasses! (74th GH records – NARA)

Alice Boehret, the 74th's second lieutenant nurse was not wholly over-enthusiastic about her new surroundings, however. The day after arriving

74th GH – Tented ward extensions. (University of Tennessee)

at Tyntesfield, she expressed perhaps a hasty opinion in a letter to her mother. On 10 May 1944, she wrote:

> *I think that we are going to like the hospital but the social life seems to be on the very, very dull side. You would think that I would be used to the dullness of army life by now. But I doubt very much if one ever gets used to the boredom.*

But a week later she wrote again:

> *This morning [18 May] as I was going on duty I happened to look up and saw our flag flying in front of headquarters. It gave you the grandest feeling to see it. I don't think that many of you at home realize how really wonderful it is to see the symbol of your country flying over foreign territory.*

With the approach of summer 1944, in addition to adding new facilities and improving existing, general housekeeping also required attention. Rapidly growing grass and weeds gave the whole area an untidy look. Local farmers kindly loaned powered and horse-drawn mowers to reduce grass height, but part-buried unseen bricks and rubble left by the builders when the plant was constructed damaged the cutters of some of the mowers. Nevertheless, large areas were patiently turned over and many tons of rubble removed; this subsequently to be used to improve roads on the site. All staff did their bit to sow large areas with lawn seed and plant beds of flowers: geraniums, asters, petunias and dahlias around the administration buildings and the flagpole, and overhanging nasturtiums to the motor pool greasing ramp. By high summer, the overall drabness of the hospital site had been transformed into a pleasant, fragrant parkland, more in keeping with the Tyntesfield estate.

Since the hospital had originally been designated a station hospital to accommodate 750 patients [834 actual], it fell short of the 1,000 bed requirements of a general hospital, so additional bed spaces were required. Moreover, with the invasion of France imminent, in the expected time available additional bed spaces could only be provided in tents. The 56th had built a number of concrete bases on which to erect tents, but more were required. Accordingly, personnel of the 74th's utilities department set about the task of increasing the bed capacity. They laid about 30,000 sq ft of concrete blocks bedded on sand, with joints filled with cement mortar, to provide a hard, acceptably level floor. Onto this new floor they pitched thirty tents to extend the wards, each of which could accommodate thirty beds. They also laid concrete pathways to connect the tented areas to their mother wards, the whole operation being completed in ten days – a remarkable achievement.

Meanwhile, essential training continued. General Hawley insisted that all medical personnel should be able to speak and write clear English so that instructions and orders to others of the professions, and to patients also, would be clear and unambiguous. He also wanted doctors and nurses to be as up-to-date as possible with procedures and techniques for treating wounds and injuries that would be sustained in battle. So all medical

74th GH – Lineup of nurses. (University of Tennessee)

74th GH – Lineup of officers. (University of Tennessee)

personnel attended courses as appropriate at British hospitals and American training centres in the UK. Some also attended a course in transfusion and shock treatment at the British Army blood supply depot at Southmead Hospital in Bristol.

By the end of May 1944, although no date for the invasion was known, all in the hospital knew that it was imminent. The pace of life quickened, and an air of expectation, albeit perhaps apprehensive, affected the lives of everyone. Although almost entirely lacking experience in caring for battle casualties, the hospital's surgical and medical staff were nonetheless ready to deal with the general surgical and medical needs of the wounded and injured shortly to arrive.

The 74th's teams specialised mostly in orthopaedics, general disease and psychological disorders, so men requiring specialist surgery outside of these disciplines were sent to other hospitals. Leading up to D-Day, most American hospitals in the UK were grouped into what were called *Hospital Centres*, with the 74th included in the 803rd Hospital Centre based in Devizes, in the county of Wiltshire. The purpose of the hospital centres was to provide facilities where all medical and surgical specialities were available in a single concentrated group. Therefore, casualties needing surgery for neuro, maxilofacial, chest and thoracic wounds and injuries, and patients with severe burns requiring plastic surgery went to hospitals within the centres where experienced, specialist surgeons were available to treat their particular injuries.

Meanwhile, the 74th continued to fulfil its role as a station hospital and treat the sick and injured from nearby posts. Among those patients referred from army units in the surrounding area were many exhibiting neuro–psychiatric symptoms. Colonel Teperson recorded:

...those coming from local units who had not been in battle were largely chronic neurotics, emotionally unstable, mentally deficient, or otherwise inadequate soldiers...

When the 74th took up residence at Tyntesfield, the number of patient referrals was already reducing as many units that had been stationed nearby transferred to marshalling-area camps close to south coast ports of embarkation in readiness for the move across to France. In addition, those recovering soldiers not needing a ward bed were transferred to convalescent hospitals elsewhere in the UK to free up beds in readiness for the expected major influx of battle casualties following the D-Day offensive. Consequently, on 11 June 1944, only 315 patients remained in the hospital.

But, having lowered its bed count in readiness for the expected battle casualties, the 74th still found space for the occasional injured local civilian. In a letter to her mother written on 3 June 1944, Alice said:

Last night a little boy was put in the bed next to me. He had a broken ankle. He is adorable. I spent most of the night up with him. Of course, this morning he cried all morning because he wanted his mother. But then who doesn't!

Chapter Six

Evacuating Casualities from Combat Zones

Although not directly connected to the story of the 74th General Hospital at Tyntesfield, the process by which casualties arrived at the hospital is, nonetheless, desirable to understand.

The book 'Medicine under Canvas – War Journal of the 77th Evacuation Hospital', succinctly sums up the role of medical personnel in time of war:

> The mission of the Medical Department of the United States Army is to keep soldiers well and able to fight, or if he is wounded or sick, to evacuate him and restore him to well-being as soon as possible.

In the years prior to the invasion of France, the American Surgeon General's Department had meticulously planned procedures for handling battle casualties to fulfil the mission of the Medical Department. Following exercises carried out on south coast beaches of England to simulate battle conditions, some using live ammunition, General Hawley and his team refined the procedures. As far as could be planned ahead of events, the procedures covered every aspect of the process from initially giving a casualty first aid to returning him to a UK hospital for comprehensive treatment.

An essential first phase of the plan was to establish on the battleground the necessary means to enable a wounded soldier to be treated as he fell, and as quickly as possible thereafter to move him to a hospital for more extensive treatment. To achieve this, medical personnel of army medical battalions and naval beach battalions would accompany the first fighting soldiers to parachute into France or land on Utah and Omaha beaches. These units would rapidly set up all the facilities necessary for handling casualties: Aid Stations, Collecting Stations and Clearing Stations.

Every soldier who went into action carried his own field-dressing pack including chemicals for antibiotic and hygienic care. When a soldier was wounded or injured, he or a fellow soldier – buddy – would administer some level of first aid, if possible. If, however, self-help was inadequate, then the soldier would need help from an *aidman, the medic*, so prominent in many American war films. The aidman would give first aid where the casualty lay, but if he required further medical attention he would be moved to an *aid station*.

At an aid station, typically set up close to the battle line, doctors and medical technicians would provide additional first aid, for example, to stop bleeding and dress wounds, and if a casualty's wounds or injuries required no further treatment, he would be returned to duty. But, if a doctor decided that a casualty needed more extensive treatment or further assessment, he would be moved by ambulance, horse and cart, litter-bearer, or walk to a *collecting station*.

At a collecting station, a medical corp doctor would examine the casualty, give further treatment if required, and return a minor casualty to his unit. More seriously injured casualties would be prepared for further evacuation by ambulance to a *clearing station*.

At a clearing station, a casualty would be triaged (sorted into categories related to the severity of his wound or injury) and given further aid if required: transfusions to combat shock, drugs to reduce suffering, and, given the relatively primitive working conditions, other treatment considered achievable to prevent permanent disability. If the examining doctor considered that a casualty could be returned to duty within a relatively short time, normally a few hours, then he would be released to rejoin his unit. If, however, the doctor considered that a casualty was no longer 'able to fight' and his wounds or injuries required further attention then he would ultimately be transferred to a fully-equipped 'evacuation (transit) hospital'. For the first few months following the invasion, such hospitals existed only in England.

Correct assessment of injuries was an essential task for doctors so that, when a casualty arrived back in England, pertinent information was immediately available to medical units receiving him. Therefore, a doctor in the clearing station would attach an EMT [Emergency Medical Tag] to the casualty's clothing. On the tag, the examining doctor would note briefly the nature of wound or injury, such as head, chest, abdomen, etc, and details and time of any drug administration. Where morphine had been given to a casualty to relieve pain, doctors often wrote the letter 'M' on his forehead using perspiration-resistant lipstick. The tag would also show whether the casualty was a litter or ambulatory case [able to walk].

Litter casualties would be further labelled as transportable or non-transportable. A transportable casualty was deemed able to safely tolerate overland transportation after landing in England before needing further medical attention. Generally, non-transportable wounded were those with severe abdominal, chest and head injuries, and compound bone fractures, needing immediate attention as soon as they reached the dockside or airfield.

However, for General Hawley and his team of medical planners, the foremost question they had to answer could be simply put but was almost impossible to answer: how many casualties should he allow for? With little historical information available to him, Hawley nonetheless had to arrive at some numbers. Estimates differed within various groups tasked with arriving at numbers, but eventually he and his team agreed on a best guess. They decided that the assault force would suffer 12% wounded on D–Day, 6.5% on D+1 and D+2, thereafter reducing proportionately. Using these percentages, they calculated that over 7,200 wounded would need to be treated and evacuated on D–Day, and another 7,800 in the following forty-eight hours. Of this total, about 3% (450) would be too severely injured to be transported any distance without essential surgery.

Hawley recognized that, until permanent medical facilities could be set up in France, the wounded and injured would need to be returned to the UK for more extensive medical care. Hawley also knew that, until French ports could be captured and made usable, or US Air Force engineers could swiftly construct airstrips, all casualties needing extensive medical care could be evacuated only by sea.

The only readily available craft in the invasion force in sufficient numbers for transporting casualties was the Landing Ship Tank [LST]. These 330 ft long ocean-going ships – the length of a football pitch – basically comprised two decks: a lower transport deck and a conventional upper deck. A flat-bottomed ship, it was designed to run up onto a beach and directly discharge its cargo of tanks and other heavy vehicles through its bow doors and ramp. And emptied of its cargo, Hawley reasoned that the LST could take on board large numbers of casualties through its bow doors and ramp in a comparatively short time. In theory, the on-hand LST was the ideal vessel for evacuating large numbers of wounded back to England, but by no stretch of imagination was it considered to be the most suitable craft in which to perform surgery. When emptied of tanks, other vehicles, men and stores, the ship rode high in the water, and, being flat-bottomed with no stabilising keel, pitched and rolled severely in all but the calmest seas; but the Americans had no option.

All 103 LSTs operated by American forces were fitted out to return casualties to England. Each vessel had three tiers of removable brackets attached to the bulkheads to support approximately 144 litters. Additionally, the tank deck could accommodate 150 more litters lashed to it, thereby providing a total capacity of 294 litter casualties. And the upper deck troop compartments could accommodate many ambulatory patients. Moreover, fifty-four of the LSTs carried equipment and medical supplies to enable surgeons and enlisted technicians to carry out surgical procedures. The other forty-nine LSTs also carried some medical supplies but fewer medical staff, and these could deal only with the less severely wounded.

At the initial planning stages, the suggested practical capacity of an LST was seventy-five litter and seventy-five ambulatory patients, but this conservative figure appears more likely to relate to the number that could be loaded before an LST, stationary in the water or with its ramp down on a beach and doors open, suffered serious damage from aircraft or shore guns. In fact, the ships often returned to England carrying many more casualties than these numbers. In addition to the LSTs, four small British hospital ships were used, but, because of their greater draft, had to anchor further out from the beaches, and transferring casualties to them proved to be difficult.

After arriving off the coast of France and as soon as the last vehicles rolled off the ramps of the surgery-designated LSTs, naval corpsmen set about converting the lower tank deck into a hospital. At the rear of the deck, they set up an operating station with table, lights, water supply, drainage plumbing and instrument-sterilizing boilers. They erected tarpaulins on simple frames around the operating station to provide some degree of privacy. They unfolded bulkhead brackets and secured them in position ready to support litters bearing their wounded. Then, with little time to relax after completing their work, the bow doors opened, the ramp dropped and the ships received their first casualties.

In the early hours and days following the landings, LSTs had to lay off the beaches until they had been cleared of mines and other obstructions. Consequently, wounded had to be taken out to the LSTs in smaller craft; the DUKW being one type extensively used. This versatile 2½-ton amphibious truck could be used conventionally as a road vehicle, and could also operate as a boat. It included six driven wheels for land use, and a propeller and rudder for operating on water. Manufactured by the General Motors Corporation, its DUKW designation, with no particular logic, derived from the manufacture's code for the type: D stood for date, 1942 – the first year of manufacture; U signified its amphibious capability; K signified drive to all wheels; and W signified dual rear axles.

In operation, with up to twelve litter cases lashed crosswise on its top, the DUKW drove down the beach to the water's edge and, without stopping, entered the water and 'swam' out to and boarded an LST via its ramp. In practice, however, with even a slight sea running, this operation was not always successful. An 'after the battle' survey showed that approximately fifty per cent of casualties had to be lifted off transporting craft using specially designed lifting gear. As American forces drove the Germans back from the beaches and gained ground, and the beaches were cleared of mines and other obstructions, LSTs ran up onto a beach, opened their bow doors, dropped their ramps and loaded all casualties directly into the tank deck.

Since LSTs on their outward trips from England mostly carried fighting vehicles, men and equipment to the beaches, they could not legitimately display red crosses to identify themselves as hospital ships when returning to England carrying casualties. Sadly, therefore, an LST was a legitimate target for German E-boats and aircraft, and, if attacked and terminally damaged, it effectively became a coffin since the chance of rescuing litter patients was nil.

DUKW loading onto LST Portland harbour in preparation for D-Day. (US Navy photograph – NARA)

Wounded being transferred onto LST-134 at Utah beach 12 June 1944. (US Navy photograph – NARA)

Wounded being transferred onto LST-134 at Utah beach 12 June 1944. (US Navy photograph – NARA)

Medical staffing of the LSTs

American Navy personnel, including their medical complement, crewed the LSTs. In keeping with its designated role in the evacuation process, the medical complement of each LST comprised three, two or one officers and twenty enlisted corpsmen. However, few of the medical officers were experienced surgeons, so General Hawley agreed to reinforce each LST medical complement with an army surgical team of one officer and two enlisted technicians, temporarily reassigned from permanent station and general hospitals.

On its day of arrival at Tyntesfield, 10 May 1944, Colonel Teperson the 74th's CO received orders from ETOUSA [European Theater of Operations United States of America] headquarters to send selected medical officers and enlisted technicians capable of performing surgery on LSTs to the 316th Station Hospital at Camp Stover, three miles outside the town of Newton Abbot, Devon. So, on 15 May 1944, a team comprising two surgeons and four medical technicians left Tyntesfield for Camp Stover to join surgical teams from other hospitals in the UK. Here, they would undergo intensive training on how to deal with casualties both on LSTs and in the clearing stations if appropriate.

The surgical teams' primary task was to stabilise a casualty and keep him alive. To this end, surgeons and their assistants would perform emergency surgery to control bleeding, including limb amputations if required; give whole blood or plasma transfusions to counter shock and loss of blood;

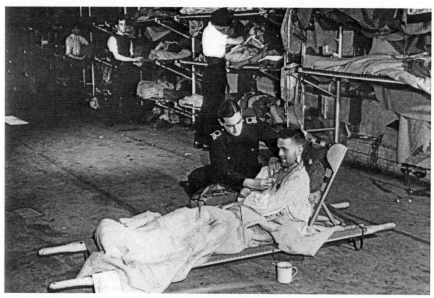

Royal Navy medical officer tending a wounded soldier aboard LST 425 in Mediterranean landings before D-Day. This shows the litters supported by brackets on the side walls. (Martin Wilson/D-Day Museum)

*Interior view of an LST tank deck showing brackets to support litters with litter wounded in place.
(US Navy photograph – NARA)*

administer pain-relieving drugs; splint broken limbs; and provide any other necessary treatment to sustain life and enable the casualty to return to England for further treatment in properly equipped hospitals. The surgeons were to carry out major surgery only to save a life, decided upon only after careful consideration of the patient's needs.

Evacuation by sea

So, by D-Day, all the procedures from initially treating a casualty on a beach or in a field and evacuating him to hospitals in the UK had been exhaustively planned and rehearsed. Everything was in place. Sadly, however, real warfare never progresses quite as planned. Some time elapsed before communications and the proper chain in the evacuation process could be fully established. Therefore, in the early chaotic days following the invasion, some casualties were taken directly to the hospital LSTs, some to be patched up and returned to the beaches, and others, needing urgent medical care including surgery, would receive their first medical attention on the sea transport returning them to England.

The journey back from French beaches to ports on the south coast of England was about seventy-five miles. Travelling at an average speed of about eight knots but hindered by necessary zigzagging to avoid detection by Luftwaffe fighters and sometimes U-boats, the trip back to England in an LST usually took about twelve hours. A not unusual trip endured by a wounded soldier can be best appreciated from the following extract of the recollections of John Absolon, a British soldier wounded by a shellburst and returned to England in July 1944:

I was taken back to the casualty evacuation centre and unloaded. At about 6pm, a decision was taken to use an LST (Landing Ship Tank). Casualties were loaded onto DUKWs (amphibious lorries), cross-wise on the top, in pouring rain, and then swam (sic) out to the LST in rough weather, salt spray drenching us. The Duck just managed to get up the ramp after two or three tries...

By about 9pm, 300 of us were on stretchers in the hold of the LST, which stunk of diesel oil (even today the smell of diesel oil takes me back to the horror of that LST). We set sail in a rough sea (the early July gales) and at about 11:30pm, once clear of the breakwaters (Mulberry Harbour), the motion became very violent.

It is almost impossible to describe the scene. Nearly dark in the hold, the smell, the stretchers sliding about, and dim figures moving from stretcher to stretcher. Being flat bottomed, the movement in the hold was terrible with water slopping about under the stretchers, and people were suffering from sea sickness. Aft – a brightly lit area with doctors working on casualties and changing dressings and trying to keep their feet as the ship rolled and the wind howled.

I was on a stretcher in the centre of the hold. Near me was a roped-off area, which everybody avoided. One patient was crying out continuously, 'The U-boats will sink us,' and one of the walking wounded was doing his best to comfort him.

Halfway across there was a tremendous crash. The wind and the rain poured in, and the twenty-ton lift for raising vehicles crashed from the top deck into the roped-off square about six feet from me. Fortunately, it didn't go through to the bottom, but I don't think many people cared one way or the other. The wind blew in and the rain poured down as the crew tried to cover the hole with tarpaulins. We were all wet, dirty, and not very happy. After some hours of this, the sea seemed to ease and I realised we were in Southampton Water.

We duly docked somewhere near Southampton. It was dark and I didn't know what day it was and I'm not sure that I cared.

Most casualties returned to England by sea arrived at one of two ports on the south coast – the vast Portland Harbour, close to Weymouth, and Southampton. Brixham, Plymouth and Falmouth were standby ports, though little used. On arrival, non-transportable severely wounded were given immediate further medical treatment in field hospitals set up on or close to the dockside. A field hospital was a semi-permanent 400-bed hospital whose role was to provide definitive surgical and medical treatment to troops in the theatre of operations where fixed facilities did not exist. This treatment ranged from stabilising a casualty using blood or plasma transfusions and administering drugs, to surgery. Such casualties were held at a field hospital until they grew strong enough to be sent to nearby evacuation hospitals, also called transit hospitals. These hospitals, usually set up in permanent buildings, were better equipped to carry out major surgery.

Injured or wounded casualties classified as 'transportable' were taken by ambulance directly from the ships to evacuation hospitals, generally within about twenty-five miles of the unloading point. Guided by the tagged information, medical staff at these hospitals reassessed the patient's needs, separated the wounded who were deemed unable to travel farther from those who could be moved, and prepared the latter cases for movement to general hospitals farther inland for more extensive treatment. The immediately transportable casualties included ambulatory patients whose only needs generally were replacement of dressings and cleaning up, or those who required further surgical attention but not immediately. Those who were not able to travel immediately received further treatment in evacuation hospitals, including surgery, and were held until they could be moved.

With casualties arriving regularly at evacuation hospitals, a rapid turnover of patients was essential. So, as soon as a casualty was considered fit enough to move on to a general hospital like the 74th, he was moved, thereby freeing up the bed for another newly arrived casualty from the battlefield. The aim was to clear the hospital of transportable casualties within forty-eight hours of arrival.

During the first eleven days of the campaign, LSTs transferred about eighty per cent of all wounded evacuated from Normandy. The average number carried per trip was about seventy-eight with the single greatest being 331. However, few ships brought back more than 200 at a time. By 5 July, 23,377 casualties had been returned to England comprising 17,247 American Army personnel, 2,078 American Navy, 1,298 allies and 2,678 German prisoners-of-war (POWs). And in the 114-day period from 6 June 1944 to 28 September 1944, LSTs transferred 41,035 wounded men back to England. Of those returned to England by LSTs and other sea craft, approximately one third were ambulatory and two thirds litter cases. After unloading their wounded in England, the LSTs then loaded medical equipment for the return trip to France to start the process again.

As Allied invasion forces advanced beyond the beaches and secured ground, the foothold on the Continent became more secure, so the Americans were able to establish more permanent field hospitals in France. In the field hospitals, essential and more extensive treatment could be performed more or less immediately; and with air evacuation gaining momentum, the need for emergency surgery on board the LSTs reduced considerably. So, by the end of June, Hawley withdrew his army surgeons and technicians from LSTs and returned them to their hospitals. Moreover, by October the allies had secured a number of French ports, the first of these being Cherbourg, so more substantial and better equipped hospital ships were able to dock, thus ending the need for LSTs as casualty carriers.

Evacuation by air

Within four days of D-Day, four days earlier than planned, American engineers had constructed airstrips close to the beaches to enable twin-engined C-47 Skytrain aircraft to evacuate casualties by air, the first flight taking off on 10 June 1944. Initially, these flights landed at either Ramsbury or Membury airfields in Wiltshire in the south of England from where thousands of American paratroopers had taken off in the same aircraft less than a week earlier. At these airfields, tented field hospitals, set up on the airfields adjacent to the runways, performed the same role as those at the reception seaports in providing instant emergency treatment.

The numbers evacuated by air grew so rapidly that between June 10 and July 31, 25,959 American wounded returned to England by plane, accounting for almost thirty-three per cent of all US casualties. As the benefits of air evacuation became apparent, the Medical Department and the Ninth United States Air Force opened additional receiving facilities at other British airfields

Wounded being transferred from a Dodge WC-54 ambulance into a C47 Skytrain in France for transfer to England. (WW2 US Medical Research Centre: www.med-dept.com)

close to general hospitals. Some casualties landed at Filton airfield, north of Bristol, though it is not recorded whether any ended up at Tyntesfield. More probably they went to the 110th General Hospital at Frenchay. The transfer time by air was considerably less than by sea, but the downside was that the C-47 carried a maximum of twenty-four litter patients compared with the LST's 300. Nonetheless, despite the fewer casualties carried on each trip, they travelled much more comfortably and arrived at hospital more quickly than by sea so further essential surgery could be performed much more promptly. An additional advantage of air evacuation was that the turnaround time for the return trip was much quicker than for LSTs. The medical services in the UK could handle 6,000 air-evacuated casualties per day but, despite the rapid allocation of additional airfields in England set up to receive casualties, even the increased capacity proved inadequate to meet all medical needs. By late September 1944, a backlog awaiting transfer from the Continent to England had grown to almost 7,000 patients.

Like LSTs, the C-47's primary role was to transport men and materials to the war zone, and returning casualties to the UK was a secondary role. Consequently, like LSTs, the aircraft could not display red crosses. General Hawley pleaded with the Air Force top brass to provide dedicated air ambulances, but his pleas were rejected because of aircraft shortage.

Hospital trains

In the early planning stages, General Hawley and his team decided that the most rapid and comfortable means of transferring casualties from near-port evacuation hospitals to general hospitals farther inland was by train. So, for patient-transfer journeys in excess of about thirty miles, trains were used wherever possible in preference to road ambulances. Each hospital train comprised from eleven to fifteen standard British coaches, customized to provide suitable accommodation for both litter and ambulatory patients. Included also was a coach for the medical staff, a pharmacy coach in which minor operations could be carried out, a boiler car for producing hot water for improved carriage heating, and a kitchen/dining car. The capacity of the trains varied depending upon type, but generally each was equipped to carry up to about 230 litter patients and sixty-four ambulatory patients, a total close to 300.

At D-Day, fifteen hospital trains, all based in south and south-west England were available to the Americans for transferring patients from near-port hospitals in Dorset, Hampshire and Devon to inland general hospitals. Patients were taken from evacuation hospitals to nearby railway stations by ambulance or coach and loaded onto the train. By the end of June 1944, eighty-four train movements had transferred approximately 23,800 casualties from early treatment evacuation hospitals to general hospitals in reasonable comfort.

So that a casualty could be transferred to hospital as quickly as possible after arriving at the railway station, the army medical department established a set procedure. Approximately twenty-five miles from a train's destination, medical staff from the hospital to which casualties were being taken boarded the train. They progressed through the train and, guided by the nature of injuries described on a casualty's tag, allocated him to a particular ward most suited to his type of injury, adding the ward number to the tag. At the railway station, ambulance crews loaded litter patients assigned to specific wards into appropriate ambulances, so that, when they arrived at hospital, they could be taken directly to the assigned ward and settled into bed as quickly as possible.

Chapter Seven

The Realities of War Arrive at the 74th

The mid-morning news broadcast by the BBC on 6 June 1944 included an announcement, long-awaited by all in Britain and the United States, and feared by the Germans:

> *This is the BBC Home Service – and here is a special bulletin read by John Snagge. D-Day has come. Early this morning the Allies began the assault on the north-western face of Hitler's European fortress. The first official news came just after half past nine, when Supreme Headquarters of the Allied Expeditionary Force issued Communiqué Number One. This said: "Under the command of General Eisenhower, Allied naval forces, supported by strong air forces, began landing Allied armies this morning on the northern coast of France."*

Six days later, on 12 June 1944, 180 casualties arrived at Bristol Temple Meads railway station. The litter cases were loaded into American Dodge and loaned Bristol ARP ambulances, four to each ambulance, and the ambulatory cases boarded British single-deck buses. The fleet of vehicles quietly rolled down the incline away from the station and headed south on its seven-mile journey. It passed through the blacked out, sleeping village of Long Ashton and turned west onto the road for Wraxall. Two miles further on, the convoy slowed and stopped, each ambulance and bus waiting on the deserted narrow country road until a military policeman directed it into the 74th General Hospital to unload its wounded. Some of the early casualties of the invasion force that had landed by sea and air in France and had been patched up on the beaches, in LSTs and then in south coast evacuation hospitals, had arrived for more definitive care and attention.

On seeing the condition of the most severely wounded, hospital staff reacted in mixed ways: some simply displayed shock, some sadness, some shed tears and all expressed fury at the extent of carnage and physical damage inflicted on their countrymen who had now become their patients.

Litter cases who arrived by ambulance were taken directly to their assigned wards, the most severely wounded sometimes accompanied by a chaplain. Casualties were settled into beds and made comfortable. Next, the

A signboard directing ambulances to Bristol Temple Meads railway station. (Author via National Trust, Tyntesfield)

WWII Dodge WC-54 ambulance.(Martin Collins)

A WWII Bristol ARP [Air Raid Precautions] ambulance. (George Morley)

ward medical officer made his rounds and, guided by the information on the casualty's tag, assessed his medical needs and classified him into one of three groups. Those requiring immediate attention, usually surgery, the doctor categorized as Group I patients and pinned a piece of bright red identifying flannel prominently to his bed covers; those who could wait a brief time for treatment the doctor assigned as Group II patients; and those whose wounds or injuries required no urgent attention the doctor assigned as Group III patients. Those patients not requiring immediate surgery were given a hot drink and food while those requiring immediate surgery and an anaesthetic received no food or drink. The needs of ambulatory patients were similarly assessed, but usually less urgently since they were generally in Groups II and III. On arrival at the hospital, ambulatory patients first reported to the receiving office where their personal details were recorded, after which they were taken to their wards. Litter patients taken directly to wards were later visited by receiving office staff who recorded personal details at their bedside.

Following surgery, casualties were transferred to nearby post-operative surgical wards. In due course, doctors and nurses next segregated patients by type of injury and allocated them to appropriate recovery wards. For example, those with fractures of the long bones of the legs and needing traction were all assigned to wards equipped for such treatment; those who had undergone amputations were assigned to common wards; and those with multiple injuries and suffering shock were moved to wards where medical staff were experienced in dealing with such conditions. Assigning wounded soldiers with similar injuries to the same wards greatly benefited them because nursing staff quickly became skilled in handling certain types of injury and disability.

Moreover, hospital staff quickly recognised that one of the most effective ways of raising an injured man's morale was to place him in a ward with other men who had received the same sort of injury and who were on the way to recovery. This was particularly true if an amputation had been performed or was thought likely. A patient who had undergone a leg amputation, for example, would probably be less upset in a ward with men of similar disabilities than with men whose only injury was a broken finger.

Hospital staff soon established the best routines for dealing with the wounded and injured soldiers in their care. They also quickly recognised that if Group III patients received early treatment then they could be released from the ward, thereby freeing up beds, and transferred to recuperation hospitals, and hopefully a quick return to their units. Therefore, special teams were assigned to these patients to speed up their recovery.

The general pattern of injuries varied somewhat as time and fighting progressed but, through the summer and autumn of 1944, the distribution of injuries suffered by soldiers arriving in general hospitals like the 74th was estimated to be: extremities, 50 per cent; abdominal, 12 per cent; thoracic, 9 per cent; thoracoabdominal, 1.5 per cent; and all other, 27.5 per cent. Nearly two thirds of all injuries subsequently treated in general hospitals were to the extremities, while multiple injuries accounted for only about 1.3 per cent. These estimates are based on the medical records of patients admitted to hospitals, so soldiers who died before reaching a hospital probably did so from severe multiple wounds or wounds to vital organs. Of the early battle casualties arriving at the 74th, many had received severe leg wounds caused by mines exploding on the beaches; others had lost arms handling and dismantling captured ammunition, some of which had been booby-trapped by the Germans; and others had suffered wounds from exploding shell fragments tearing into their bodies.

As the Allies advanced through France and Belgium, many casualties arrived at the 74th suffering from non-battle injuries. As seaports captured from the Germans became available, war supplies could be more efficiently unloaded using proper port facilities. American port battalions provided labour at these ports, and thousands of soldiers from these units suffered serious non-combat injuries of bones, joints and soft tissues. Many other soldiers suffered injuries in road traffic accidents.

But not all admitted to the 74th needed only surgical or medical treatment. In the period from 10 May to 31 December 1944, the hospital admitted 526 soldiers diagnosed with neuro-psychiatric disorders. Of these, only a few had been admitted prior to D-Day from units based within the hospital's catchment. Most had arrived from the fighting in France in an 'acute anxiety state'. [In WWI this was called 'shell shock'; today it is called 'post traumatic stress disorder' – PTSD.] But from the hospital's viewpoint, the combat-exhausted soldier, whether wounded or not, required attention just as much as the soldier otherwise wounded. When casualties arrived at the 74th, some clearly exhibited combat-exhaustion symptoms necessitating special management. For these, medical staff frequently sought the opinion of a psychiatrist if emotional disturbances were apparent. As time passed, however, specialist psychiatric services were needed less because surgeons, after handling large numbers of such patients, had themselves gained experience in managing them. Of all the medical service divisions within the hospital, excluding surgical, the neuro-psychiatric section accounted for the greatest number of patients. Eventually, two thirty-bed wards were needed to accommodate this type of patient, and specially trained nurses and enlisted men with peacetime experience cared for them.

Not only battle casualties occupied the beds in wards of the 74th. Patients suffering from commonplace medical problems also needed beds. Many of these suffered from catarrh, bronchial problems and laryngitis and, in the cold damp British climate, these ailments proved to be more resistant to treatment. Acute upper respiratory infections predominated in the spring, decreasing in the summer months and increasing again with the coming of autumn and winter. And rheumatic fever and arthritis also responded less well to treatment in Britain than in the warmer states of America.

Dermatological and VD patients also occasionally needed bed spaces and specialised attention. To accommodate this class of patient, one 32-bed ward was specifically allocated.

From time to time female patients needed medical attention and nursing, so the 12-bed ward originally allocated for accommodating infectious-disease patients was reallocated as a female only ward. One notable patient was nurse Alice Boehret. In early November 1944, Alice developed atypical (viral) pneumonia. For ten days from 6 November she remained on a critically ill list, receiving penicillin injections six times daily and oxygen to assist with breathing. Her condition was so severe that the hospital sent a telegram to her mother warning her that her daughter might not survive. But survive she did, though was unable to resume her duties until the middle of December. A colleague, nurse Helen Washinger-Peterson ('Wash'), dedicated herself to looking after Alice and they became close friends.

Despite a soldier's sometimes urgent need for attention, certain procedures were customarily carried out only by male medical technicians and rarely by female nurses – to avoid embarrassing either the soldier or his nurse. Patients who had undergone surgery in the area of the rectum – for the removal of haemorrhoids, for example – or required an enema, or who needed treatment to ease the discomfort of bladder infections and inflammatory bowel diseases bathed in what was called a *sitz* bath. [A *sitz* bath, also called a hip bath, was a type of bath in which only the hips and buttocks were immersed in water or a saline solution.] Alice Boehret recalls that nurses never went into the ablutions area of a ward when patients were having a *sitz* bath.

And, except in an emergency, nurses did not normally enter male wards containing soldiers suffering from Buerger's disease. This disease, seen mostly in men aged twenty to forty, resulted almost exclusively from excessive

74th GH nurse Alice Boehret and friend 'Wash' – Helen Washinger-Peterson. (University of North Carolina)

cigarette smoking. In WWII, many soldiers smoked heavily. The disease, mainly seen in the legs but sometimes in the arms, caused a progressive decrease in blood flow to the affected limbs. The restricted blood flow, or in extreme cases no blood flow at all, often caused gangrene to develop necessitating limb amputation.

Alice Boehret recalls:

I was not allowed in the ward with them [the patients]. We always took the sergeant, and he gave the instructions in Buerger's disease. In Buerger's disease the feet had to go up in the air, and they had to wave their legs and do things. So we weren't allowed in the wards; they might expose themselves!

Throughout the days following the initial landings, the Allies captured many German soldiers, some of them wounded or otherwise injured. Under the terms of the Geneva Convention relating to the treatment of wounded prisoners of war, they were regarded simply as wounded soldiers, regardless of nationality. Consequently, in the LSTs returning to England, Allied wounded often shared the accommodation with wounded German POWs, some eventually ending up in wards of the 74th.

Alice in a letter to her mother dated 25 June 1944:

Today I made rounds on the wards and saw all types of patients, friends and foe alike. One had his bottom shot off. Our boys sure know where to aim.

After the initial influx of casualties, the hospital settled into a well-organised routine and, after treatment, recovering patients moved on to convalescent hospitals to free up beds. As the census dropped and beds became available, new trainloads of patients arrived at roughly two-week intervals. By the end of September 1944, the 74th had admitted 3,194 casualties from eleven trainloads. Of these, 2,267 had sustained battle injuries, 588 suffered from various diseases, and 339 had sustained non-battle injuries.

In the four months following the first intake of battle casualties, ambulance crews had honed their skills and procedures for unloading 300 casualties from hospital trains so that they were able to complete the transfer of litter cases into ambulances and ambulatory cases into buses in forty-five minutes. One difficulty the Americans experienced, however, was the shortage of ambulances since each ambulance could transport only four litter cases in any one run. To overcome this problem, the local Bristol ARP [Air Raid Precautions] loaned ambulances and crews. But although ARP ambulances could also carry only four patients, the increase in ambulance numbers enabled all wounded and injured to be transferred in one convoy.

At this stage of the war, ARP ambulances were not much needed since the last Luftwaffe air raid over Bristol and the West Country had been on the morning of 16 May 1944.

The approach of winter

With the end of Luftwaffe activity over the Bristol area, due principally to the unsustainable losses it suffered owing to its need to crew planes with inexperienced airmen, maintaining the blackout became unnecessary. Consequently, on 17 September 1944, the British authorities lifted blackout regulations, and the utilities department strung up lights along the walkways enabling hospital staff to move less hazardously between buildings in the dark hours.

By late autumn, with winter approaching, improving conditions in the tented extensions to some of the wards became necessary. In his end of year report for 1944, Colonel Teperson recorded:

> *With the coming of cold weather it was necessary to winterise all of our ward tents. This was accomplished by the installation of a fibre wall on a wooden framework along the inner surface of the tent apron. Small vestibules were also constructed at the entrance. Glass windows in the doors permitted sufficient daylight to enter the tent and eliminated the perpetual blackout which exists in tents without windows.*
>
> *An innovation which has proven most satisfactory was the erection of two ward tents side by side as a single unit. The adjoining side walls of the tents were fastened together with ropes through their opposite gromets. The aprons were then rolled up together and held in place by tying the tent wall tapes together. This adjoining partition rose to a height of approximately six feet above the floor. Thirty beds could be accommodated in three rows of ten with the middle row beneath the junction of the two tents. This left two wide isles for easy passage.*

Despite these measures, with almost no natural daylight and only two stoves to heat them, living conditions in the tents remained grim. Generally, only ambulatory patients occupied the tented extensions to the wards, spending their daytime hours in the recreation or clubrooms, chatting to other patients confined to bed, strolling around the hospital complex or the Tyntesfield estate, and returning only to the tents to sleep. In adjacent beds, patients slept head to foot; that is, a patient in one bed slept with his head at one end of the bed while the patient in the adjacent bed slept with his feet at the same end so they wouldn't breathe in each other's face.

And into November, as the temperature fell, the continuing struggle to keep warm became even more of a concern to hospital staff. The cast-iron 'tortoise' stoves in most of the wards and living quarters never wanted to stay alight through the night, especially when fuelled with coke. In the wards, heated only by three stoves, enlisted men kept them topped up but in living quarters, the residents usually took turns to get up every two hours or so throughout the night to add fuel in an effort to keep the stoves alight.

One unidentified enlisted soldier commented about his sleeping quarters:

> *The wind whistled through gaps in the walls, while the stoves tried in vain to keep up the room temperature.*

December brought no respite, being mainly cold throughout with a hard frost and fog later in the month. And January 1945 added further misery to the hospital staff with frequent snowfalls blanketing the countryside for eleven days of the month. For the nurses in hut 102, their toilet was 150 yards up a slight hill from their hut. And in the night with snow falling and the temperature below freezing, few were prepared to put on boots and clothes to visit the toilet, so some of them relieved themselves near to their hut. Alice Boehret recalls:

> *...and the bathroom was up a hill, about four huts up. So in the morning there were little yellow holes in the snow outside the door.*

Following the arrival of the eleventh train on 23 September 1944, the intake of wounded at the 74th slowed appreciably and, by the end of November, only three further trains carrying wounded and injured soldiers arrived at Temple Meads station, the last being on 29 November 1944. This trainload of patients would be the last that year for, on 3 December 1944, the American authorities redesignated Tyntesfield as a 'holding hospital' for patients to be repatriated to the United States.

Nonetheless, the work rate of the hospital slackened little as medical teams continued, seven days a week, to mend and nurse the broken bodies of the

74th GH – Ward 14 staff posing in snow January 1945. (University of Tennessee)

104

latest arrivals. In the operating rooms, surgeons and their assistants stayed at operating tables for as long as a patient needed their skills; and, in the wards, nurses and enlisted men continued to work their twelve-hour or longer shifts, snatching sleep whenever they could. But once this last intake of patients had been taken care of, and with the change of designation, numbers of patients admitted from nearby units and other hospitals requiring surgical and medical attention slowed appreciably, and most of the work entailed changing plaster casts and dressings. The administrative branch of the hospital saw a marked increase in their work, however, updating medical records of new arrivals destined for return to the States.

Despite the unrelenting work, the 74th managed to celebrate Christmas in the traditional way. Although no copy of the menu could be located, the fare provided was likely to be similar to that enjoyed by the 56th the previous Christmas. Alice Boehret in a letter to her mother, written on 29 December 1944, said:

> *Christmas was very nice. I think I would have been very homesick if I had not been in the hospital. Jonesy [role not known] had spent a good deal of effort to make the table very attractive and we all sat around it and enjoyed ourselves. I of course had on my white uniform and Jeff cap so naturally I had to sit at the head of the table. There was plenty of turkey and celery so I hid some away for my usual Christmas night supper. I think I would have felt terrible if I couldn't have had my turkey and celery sandwich. [Jeff cap refers to her nurse's cap awarded at Jefferson Medical College Hospital School of Nursing, Philadelphia where she trained from 1938 to 1941.]*

The end of 1944 arrived with the 74th having admitted a total of 4,167 patients from evacuation hospitals farther south. Of that number, 2,823 were battle casualties, 870 general diseases and 474 accidental non-battle casualties. In the period to the end of 1944, of all admissions, including those from local units in training, 526 patients were suffering from miscellaneous neuro-psychiatric disorders. The majority responded in varying degrees to treatment, but few returned to their original units.

Staffing levels remained fairly constant during 1944 except for nurses whose numbers gradually reduced as the year progressed. Of the 100 nurses who first arrived at Tyntesfield, 21 transferred to other hospitals or left for other un-stated reasons. At midnight on 31 December 1944, personnel in the hospital numbered: surgical and medical corps – 33 officers and 1 warrant officer; dental corps – 5 officers; nurses – 9; dieticians – 2; physical therapy aids – 2; enlisted men – 490; and civilians 67, most of whom were part-time volunteers.

The war grinds on into 1945

Allied forces steadily progressed through France, Belgium and Holland and, by the middle of September 1944, straddled the Belgium/German border at the Hürtgen Forest in the south-west corner of the German Federal State of North Rhine-Westphalia. Meanwhile, Russian forces unremittingly fought their way towards Germany from the East.

From D-Day onwards, the German army fought an essentially defensive battle, retreating before the advancing Allies. But, at the Hürtgen forest, only fifty square miles in area, the Germans stiffened their resistance and the American advance effectively ground to a halt. From 14 September 1944 to 10 February 1945, the Americans fought a series of fierce battles, advancing little. These battles collectively became known as the *Battle of Hürtgen Forest*, costing the Americans at least 33,000 killed, wounded or injured, including both combat and non-combat losses. And the Americans were to suffer many more casualties elsewhere in a five-week period during December and January.

While opposing armies fought in the Hürtgen Forest, Adolph Hitler, the German leader, convinced himself that the alliance between the United Kingdom, France and America in the western sector of Europe was not strong and that a major attack and defeat would break up the alliance. So he planned a massive offensive against the Allies that would, in his mind, destabilise their accord. His primary aim was to recapture the important port of Antwerp through which, from 28 November, large quantities of war materials arrived to supply the Allies. Therefore, he ordered a massive attack against what were primarily American forces in an area of Belgium known as the Ardennes Forest. On the night of 16 December 1944, the German Army launched its attack, officially known as the *Ardennes Offensive* but more popularly known as the *Battle of the Bulge* because the initial attack by the Germans created a bulge in the Allied front line. The battle raged for five weeks with little movement on either side, and the Allies did not gain the upper hand and start to move forward until 27 January 1945.

At the time, Belgium and most of mainland Europe was experiencing the coldest winter for thirty years with frequent heavy snowfalls, and deep-lying snow and frost persisting for many weeks. Tens of thousands of soldiers were stranded for days in foxholes – shallow depressions and trenches carved out of the frozen ground – and these rapidly became waterlogged. Unable to move out of the waterlogged holes, soldiers suffered from prolonged exposure to cold and wet and developed what was called 'cold injury, ground type'. These injuries were further classed into three groups: trench foot, frostbite and immersion foot. Trench foot was caused by prolonged exposure of feet to cold at just above freezing temperature; frostbite was caused by exposure to cold at and below freezing temperatures; and immersion foot was caused by prolonged exposure of feet in cold water. Cold injury constricted small blood vessels, cutting off or restricting blood supply to the feet, resulting in the small blood vessels and nerve endings becoming permanently damaged. Feet became numb and swelled painfully, often culminating in tissue death and gangrene. These injuries were as much the enemy as German troops for American soldiers.

In some circles within the American army, it was believed that the push across Europe would proceed relatively unhindered and that the war would be over before the 1944 winter set in. But the belief was ill-founded. Historically, in modern times no major military campaigns had been fought in Western Europe during cold winter months. So the army medical hierarchy, although vaguely aware of the need for a soldier to keep his feet in good condition, but with no experience of the medical and military aspects of 'cold trauma', gave scant consideration to providing the ground soldier with winter clothing, footgear and other winterising equipment. Instead, top priority was given to transporting ammunition, gasoline and other combat requirements to the front to the exclusion of winter clothing and footgear.

But, just in case the need arose, shortly before D-Day the medical hierarchy did issue guidelines to soldiers about how to look after their feet, though their recommendations were quite ridiculous. They recommended that, after exposure to cold and moisture, he should bathe his feet in a footbath with soap and water, massage for twenty minutes and then change into dry socks and shoes. But, after spending many hours in a cold, wet hole in the ground dodging enemy mortar shells and other ordnance, the soldier's main concern was to avoid having his head blown off. Advice about how to care for his feet was not exactly uppermost in his thoughts.

At the time, GI field shoes and combat boots were totally inappropriate for winter conditions since they were fitted in warmer months of the year and were too small to allow a soldier to wear more than one pair of socks without unduly constricting his feet. In his foxhole, with no means of drying boots or drying or replacing his socks, the wretched soldier suffered severely from the damp and freezing conditions.

One American soldier's platoon started out with forty-two men and only eight survived. He recalls:

If a man was hit and fell, the medics had only 20 minutes to find him in the snow before he froze to death. There were continual artillery barrages, both incoming and outgoing. Men suffered from frozen feet, frostbite, trench foot, battle fatigue and pneumonia in addition to dealing with the battle casualties. Unit commanders got little or no sleep. Soldiers were exposed to the elements day and night – always cold, always hungry and always frightened.

But even when hospitalised, a soldier could not be assured of full recovery. At the time, treatment was speculative; the medical profession simply did not know how to provide definitive treatment. A widely held view was that stimulating blood flow to the affected feet would help to repair the damage. One method practised at some general hospitals, including the 74th, was to give soldiers a shot of whisky every three hours or so to encourage blood flow in the damaged vessels. Whether this helped is conjectural, but the warm glow may have helped the soldier feel less miserable. Other than shots of whisky, treatment was to confine the patient to bed and keep him warm generally, but to expose and elevate his damaged foot or feet. And, as with recovery from most injuries, the suffering soldier was encouraged to walk as soon as he was able.

The Battle of the Bulge was largely an American battle; some 600,000 soldiers fought it and 80,000 were killed, wounded or captured. In the American Third Army, for every ten men evacuated, six suffered from various forms of cold injury. Between November 1944 and April 1945, more than 45,000 were hospitalised as cold-injury casualties. Any sort of recovery was not speedy; a soldier being treated for severe cold injury would be out of action, usually for between forty-five and seventy days. Even after hospital treatment, of those casualties who eventually emerged with feet intact, only about fifteen per cent ever returned to their units to fight again because their feet ached from marching and were very sensitive to cold.

Although designated as a holding hospital during the Battle of the Bulge fighting, the 74th nonetheless took its share of patients from that battle with close to 300 new wounded arriving by train on 30 January, and further similar numbers on 12 February and 6 March 1945. Two thirds of the casualties arriving on these three trains were classed as surgical cases, while most of the remainder suffered from cold injuries. Alice Boehret recalls:

> We got an awful lot of frozen feet in. I can remember taking my bandage scissors and cutting toes off because they were frozen through and only the rest was hanging and it was all dead [sic].

In the last few months leading up to the end of the war, the 74th also admitted a number of Allied prisoners-of-war, known as RAMPs [Recovered Allied Military Personnel]. Few required extensive medical or surgical treatment, though some were suffering from respiratory problems. Most simply required a good bath, general care and good food to satisfy their voracious appetites and rebuild their strength.

As the drive across Europe into Germany became fully established, the American Medical Department set up more fully equipped general and station hospitals on mainland Europe, so the intake of patients by the 74th reduced over the last few months of the war.

Alice Boehret again in a letter to her mother dated 27 April 1945:

We are still very busy. Every one is restless because the work we are doing isn't the easiest to do. All our patients are waiting for the boat and that doesn't help our morale any. Almost all the work is administrative.

The war in Europe ends

Despite the temporary setback to Allied progress caused by the Ardennes Offensive, the war's outcome was inevitable, accepted even by the more rational thinking Germans. Albert Speer, Germany's Reich Minister for Armaments and War Production wrote at the time:

The failure of the Ardennes Offensive meant that the war was over.

Albert Speer's words were prophetic for at 3:00 pm on Tuesday 8 May 1945, from his residence at 10 Downing Street, London, the British Prime Minister Winston Churchill broadcast to the world:

Yesterday morning at 2:41 am at General Eisenhower's headquarters, General Jodl, the representative of the German High Command and of Grand Admiral Doenitz, the designated head of the German State, signed the act of unconditional surrender of all German land, sea, and air forces in Europe to the Allied Expeditionary Force, and simultaneously to the Soviet High Command.

Hostilities will end officially at one minute after midnight tonight (Tuesday, May 8), but in the interests of saving lives the "Cease fire" began yesterday to be sounded all along the front, and our dear Channel Islands are also to be freed today.

Victory in Europe had been achieved.

Although the staff of the 74th celebrated with the rest of Europe and the United States, they still had a hospital to run and patients to look after. At that date, 1,030 patients remained in their care. The hospital continued to perform its role as a station hospital for the few remaining units within its catchment, and to hold patients awaiting ships for return to the United States.

In a letter to mother written on 10 May 1945, Alice wrote:

It doesn't seem possible that the war in Europe is over. The English have had two days of holiday. The women that work in the ward kitchen only had one day. We got an extra hour on Tuesday but that is all. Of course we haven't settled back to normal yet and I doubt if we really grasp the fact even yet.

Speech by CO of 74th GH in front of flag. The occasion unknown, but possibly at the end of the war. (74th GH records – NARA)

Nonetheless, with less work generally, hospital staff were allowed more time for leisure, and to prepare for eventual return to civilian life. On 18 May 1945, hospital management set up an *Information and Education* (I & E) group which organised a number of leisure trips for many of the hospital personnel. Parties visited Cheddar and Bath on 1 June; Cardiff on 8 June; and the nearby Long Ashton Research Station on 12 June to learn about its work in researching and cultivating fruits, particularly apples, pears, plums, strawberries and blackcurrants.

But finally, its work coming to an end, the hospital closed at midnight on 21 May 1945 after which it accepted no new admissions. During its wind-down period, in appreciation of the work done by local women volunteers, the American Red Cross organised a party for them on 4 June 1945 attended by approximately thirty-five of the volunteers. And through the month following its closure, many items, including personal belongings of the staff, were packed in readiness for their departure from Tyntesfield.

In her final letter dated 22 June 1945 written at Tyntesfield to sister Dorothy, Alice wrote:

> *Jerry [another nurse] and I have been sitting here trying to decide if anyone at home would ever believe that American girls could live as we are right now. I seriously doubt it. We can hardly believe it ourselves. Of course, anyone standing back and looking at it objectly [sic] would split*

their sides laughing because it is simply hilariously funny.

Picture fourteen women whose ages range from 43 to 22 living in one hut. All they have to live with are the bare essentials. And everyone is planning to throw away their underwear she is wearing at this time. What we are wearing could never be called lingerie. Most of it is the GI khaki variety. When it comes time to lay the body horizontal another problem comes to the fore. We have no sheets or pillowcases and we have only one lone GI blanket. The problem: How can you use one blanket to do the work of three you are used to? The solution: Put on your sleeping garment (these I will describe later), add bed socks, then your sweater, your liner [?], lay the blanket on the bed the wrong way. You then lay the body in the middle of the blanket and turn the sides over you to make three thicknesses – one under and two over. Over this you drape your field coat, and believe it or not, you aren't cold.

The sleeping garments are out of this world, and I don't mean perhaps. One girl – the captain – in her confusion packed all her nightgowns and she sleeps in a lovely green chintz housecoat plus the other stuff I have previously mentioned. Then there is the new child [nurse?] who wears pyjamas and long johns on top of that.

Of course we are slightly barmy from staying in all the time. All our money has been converted to Francs and never have any of us have been so broke. If we don't move soon we will be completely psycho.

74th GH - Bristol's Lord Mayor presents the city's coat-of-arms to Col. Teperson, Commanding Officer, who in turn, presents the hospital insignia to the Lord Mayor – 17 May 1945. (University of Tennessee)

Then, for the last time, at 5:00 am on Tuesday 26 June 1945, lorries rolled out of the gates of Tyntesfield carrying the hospital's personnel. This last journey was to take them to Bristol Temple Meads station and eventual redeployment on continental Europe.

In his report covering the hospital's time at Tyntesfield, Col Teperson wrote these final comments:

> *In leaving the UK, we must consider ourselves fortunate in having been located in the vicinity of Bristol. During our slightly more than a year of operation, mutual cooperation was developed to a high degree. The Medical Officer of Health placed at our disposal a fleet of ARP ambulances for transport of patients both to and from the hospital at all hours of the day or night.*
>
> *80 British women served as volunteers on our wards under the auspices and directions of our Red Cross unit. Various British committees furnished hospitality to both staff and patients.*

Statistics Summary

After the war's end, when statistics became available and analysed, the following facts emerged: Of all patients admitted to hospitals in England, 72.4 per cent were wounded, 19.9 per cent were suffering from some form of disease including mental disorders, and 7.7 per cent were suffering from non-battle injuries. And the American Army Medical Department could be rightly proud of its achievements. If a casualty survived his injuries long enough to enter the medical treatment system, his survival chances were excellent – the death rate ran at only 2.5 per cent, comparing favourably with the 1.5 per cent who died in hospitals in the Vietnam conflict over twenty-five years later. However, of those who lived, only 14 per cent returned from army treatment facilities to front-line duty, the remainder eventually being drafted to non-combat roles or returned to the United States.

The following summary covers the period that the 74th operated at Tyntesfield; that is, from 10 May 1944 to 26 June 1945, but with limited dental service information.

Admissions

Transfer from 56th GH	416
From hospital trains	4,803
Miscellaneous (other hospitals, local other units)	2,818
Admitted for expected return to United States	13,765
Of all the admissions:	
Battle casualties numbered	10,866
Injuries numbered	3,187
Disease (including NP patients) numbered	7,749

Dispositions

Returned to duty	3,948
Transferred (for specialist surgery & convalescence)	2,309
Returned to United States	15,619
Died	13
Dead on arrival	3
Absent without leave	10

By far the greatest number of patients returned to the United States from the 74th were surgical cases, predominantly orthopaedic, the next largest being soldiers who had suffered from trench foot and other cold injuries.

Highest census (30 January 1945)	1,377
Lowest census (11 June 1944)	315

Outpatients

Visits	6,865
Treatments	10,584

Dental

Records for this department are available for the period until 31 December 1944 only. The CO's report for 1945 at Tyntesfield states that, as most of the patients for that year were waiting to be returned to the United States and spent relatively little time in the hospital, their dental needs were not routinely assessed, emergency treatment only being given. However, the following information was recorded for the department:

Examinations	4,254
Permanent fillings	5,020
Extractions	1,029
Full dentures made and fitted	77
Partial dentures made and fitted	702
Acrylic eyes made and fitted	30

Chapter Eight

Casualty Aftercare and Rehabilitation

In the early days of medical care in army hospitals in WWII, the 56th and 74th included, some surgeons considered their job done when they could confidently expect their patient to live and, from the clinical viewpoint, his wounds or injuries would heal. They soon learned, however, just how important aftercare was and how significant attention to this aspect of care contributed to prompt recovery and rehabilitation. As soon as possible after surgery, the surgeon in charge would explain to his patient as simply as possible the nature of his injury; the treatment already carried out or proposed; and how long the course of treatment would be. He would stress that the length of convalescence would depend upon his cooperation as much as upon the skill of the medical staff treating him. If he had the kind of injury that would require his return to the United States, he was told at once, though never if there was the slightest doubt that this would happen.

From the moment he could move in bed, the patient's doctor and physiotherapy technician encouraged him to engage in a programme of exercises

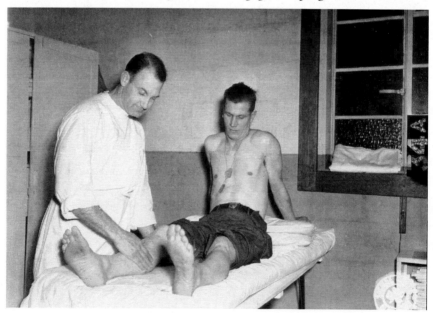

74th GH – physiotherapist working on leg of wounded soldier 3 November 1944. (Dr. Sanders Marble)

to maintain muscle tone which would otherwise wither from disuse and delay recovery. Great emphasis was placed on self-help, but also included sessions with the patient's physiotherapist.

Lt Col Philip S Foisie, a surgeon with the 129th General Hospital at Penley, ten miles from Wrexham in North Wales, wrote a booklet explaining the importance of exercise to aid recovery. It was called 'FRACTURE FACTS for the patients who GET ALL THE BREAKS'. Its recommendations are as applicable today as they were then, and are worth reproducing in full:

You have arrived at a GENERAL HOSPITAL where your broken bones and your wounds are to receive the best possible treatment we can give. The personnel of this hospital are eager to do their level best to restore full functions to your injured parts.

We will set your bones and sew up your wounds and give you medicine and take care of your needs. But your muscles are controlled by your brain alone, and WE can't move them for you any more than we could breathe for you. YOU alone have control over those muscles.

The human body is designed for continued use. It doesn't build up strength by resting, that is, not by complete rest or TOTAL inactivity. You can't pull the main switch for a month or two and then start again. The human body must function at least in low gear to stay in good condition. Muscles, particularly, depend on use to REMAIN HEALTHY. Use develops them, but with disuse they soften and shrivel up. Joints also, even uninjured ones, become stiff if they aren't moved. Wounds in healing contract or shorten so that fingers, knees, elbows, and all other joints become bent.

Therefore, if you just lie in bed and vegetate until your injuries are healed, you will have stiffened and bent-up joints which your disused muscles won't be able to straighten out again. The only way to keep your joints and muscles supple is to never let them get stiff.

Now, broken bones have to be SPLINTED in order to knit together. This means that for a while the adjacent joints will not move. We don't like this, but we can't avoid it. However, we'll tie up these joints for the shortest possible time consistent with healing. We'll watch the fractures with X-rays (and otherwise) and remove the splints as soon as we can. During this period, you can still keep the muscles strong by 'SETTING' them even though they don't actually move the joints. The ward personnel will show you how to do this.

All joints that are not tied up must be kept moving. Move everything that is not tied down. This means that if your wrist is in a splint, keep on moving your fingers and elbow and shoulder. If your middle finger is tied up, move your thumb and other fingers, and your wrist etc., and move them not just a LITTLE WIGGLE, but over the full range of motion.

Five minutes out of every hour throughout the day must be spent in setting muscles and in exercising joints. Then when a joint is removed from fixation, you are going to have to limber it up. Don't be discouraged when you find out that it won't move at first, and don't try to do it all the first day. It takes days, weeks, and sometimes months to get full motion, but this is done by constantly, hour by hour, gaining a fraction of a degree at a time, which adds up to a full range of motion.

Every one on the surgical service from technician on the ward to the Chief of Surgery on rounds will be constantly urging you to move those joints. Don't say 'I can't. IT HURTS ME.' They know that. If you do it gradually but constantly, it won't hurt very much, and even if it does, it has to be done. The more you postpone it, the harder it will be to do. The test of a good result is whether you are in BETTER shape when you are discharged from the hospital than before you got hurt.

We want good results as much as you do and we'll help you all we can, but there are some things only you can do, so, keep 'em moving and we'll all be happy.

In many American hospitals throughout the UK, believed to include the 74th, three times daily at 10:00 am, 2:00 pm and 4:00 pm, the exercise-supervising doctor would enter the ward and announce that, for the next five minutes, all non-vital activities would stop. In this period, trained physiotherapy technicians and nurses encouraged and helped patients to perform their prescribed exercises.

Fully ambulatory patients also embarked upon programmes that included walking and drilling, callisthenics and other exercises tailored to the nature of their specific needs; and those who could move around a little were encouraged to walk. It was a not uncommon site to see patients in their red dressing gowns wandering around the grounds of the Tyntesfield Estate, some even with bandaged heads and some aided by crutches.

Many bed-bound patients and some semi-ambulatory were confined to their wards, and depression was rarely far away. Workers in the rehabilitation section, workers in the various special services and American Red Cross workers all endeavoured to keep their patients occupied and leave them with no time to brood. They worked tirelessly in lending a ready ear to resolve a patient's worries, sometimes major and sometimes only seemingly major because of the circumstances. And the chaplains were always on hand to provide compassionate support to those casualties who had survived with disabilities and deformities, and also, sadly, to perform their duties for those who did not survive.

One of the highly favourable factors in treating wounded or injured soldiers and their ultimate recovery was that they were mostly men who were young, in excellent health and generally well fed.

Identity card and pin of Edith May Stokes, volunteer Red Cross worker with 74th General Hospital. (Edith Stokes via Norman Searle)

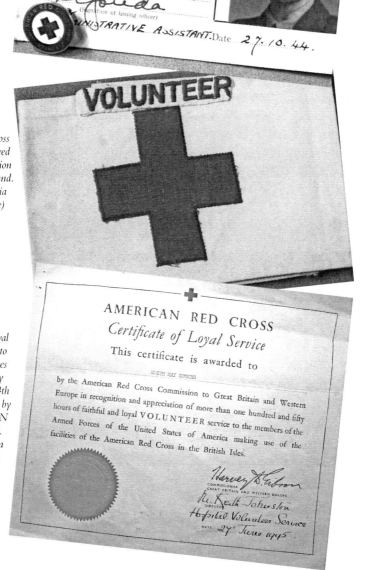

Armband of volunteer Red Cross workers – Blood-red cross and designation on white background. (Edith Stokes via Norman Searle)

Certificate of Loyal Service awarded to Edith May Stokes for her voluntary work with the 74th General Hospital by the AMERICAN RED CROSS. (Edith Stokes via Norman Searle)

Local volunteers

As soon as the hospital opened, many local women volunteered their time to help in any way they could. Although the 56th employed civilians in various roles, no record can be found that it took on local people to assist the Red Cross workers. The 74th, however, did employ a number of local ladies. Among those were Gladys Doddrell who, with three other volunteers Kay Sampson, Bonnie Ogden and Vi Wakeham, travelled by bus to the hospital from their homes in the nearby town of Nailsea. Another local lady who gave her time at the hospital in various roles was Edith Stokes. They wore no uniforms and were identified only by a white armband bearing a cross and the legend 'VOLUNTEER' in blood red, and their official passes.

For all patients, with their homes and families thousands of miles away, their only contact was by letter or sometimes a message passed on by a soldier or hospital worker repatriated to the States or returning on leave or to other duties. American Red Cross workers wrote letters home for those who had lost hands and arms, and read and wrote letters for the sightless wounded. In this role, they were greatly assisted by the local women volunteers who so willingly gave their time.

From about August 1944, Gladys Doddrell, twenty-nine years old, worked in one of the surgical wards of the 74th. Like her American counterparts, she distributed books, newspapers and magazines from her trolley to the wounded soldiers and chatted with them in their beds. She read letters to those who had lost their sight or whose eyes were bandaged; and she wrote letters for those who had lost arms or hands. Gladys recalls her embarrassment on occasions knowing a soldier's intimate business. She sewed the Purple Heart ribbon onto uniforms of American servicemen who had been injured in battle until 'her fingers bled'. Gladys remembers that, on one occasion, she was pushing her trolley of books and magazines in a surgical ward when she came upon a twenty-one year-old soldier who had been severely wounded. The sight of his appalling injuries distressed her intensely and she was violently sick, the mess to be cleaned up by a compassionate ward nurse. Gladys was so upset and emotionally affected by the experience that the authorities transferred her to a recovery ward where the sight of soldiers' wounds and injuries was less emotionally disturbing.

Gladys was full of praise for the Americans at the hospital, both staff and patients. She says that hospital staff were always pleasant and generous. On a number of occasions, she was given gum and candies by staff in the PX to take home for her young daughter, born early in the war. Although she did not develop a close relationship with any of the wounded soldiers, she said that they were always greatly appreciative of the kind words and help that the volunteer ladies gave them. Gladys said that, overall, she found the whole experience worthwhile and rewarding, much better than staying at home doing nothing of consequence.

Another civilian volunteer, Freda Vowles, helped out in one of the ward kitchens, doing whatever was necessary when food arrived, and afterwards cleaning and stacking dishes. She recalls that, in conversation with one of the ward staff, she mentioned that her grandmother had a birthday coming up, and later she was given a hamper for her grandmother made up in the main food preparation kitchen. It included butter, peanut butter, fruit juices, tinned fruit and other food items. She had to sign for it so that at the gate when she went out the guard would not think she had stolen it.

Winnie Shortman also helped out in one of the ward kitchens from the beginning of 1945 to the hospital's closure. While working in the ward, she met and became friendly with Jim Carter, the medical technician. Jim recalls:

I was assigned to Ward 14 on the top of the hill near the Tyntesfield Estate. Also assigned to Ward 14 as a civilian employee was a young lady named Winifred Shortman. I remember her when we first met as being so vivacious and sweet. Little did I know she would be my future wife.

After VE day [Victory in Europe – 8 May 1945] the 74th departed Tyntesfield on June 26, 1945 and crossed the channel to France. St. Quentin, Commercy, Nancy, and Metz are some of the places where we were stationed.

After I was discharged from the army, I returned to England for visits. My visit in 1958 was the greatest for then I married Winifred Shortman in Nailsea and brought her to America.

Wedding of Jim Carter and Winnie Shortman. (Jim Carter via Nailsea & District Local History Society)

Their story is taken up by Winnie:

I worked at the 74th Gen Hospital for the last six months they were at Tyntesfield. After VE day the outfit was transferred to France. Before Jim left he said he would write to me from France and let me know how they were doing. From then on we continued writing. Several times Jim came to England for visits and I went to USA one time. Back then we travelled on the Cunard Queens, Elizabeth and Mary.

We were married on April 2nd 1958 at The Methodist Chapel in Silver St., Nailsea. We left Southampton on the Queen Elizabeth, April 10th and arrived in New York on April 15th. After visiting with Violet Summerell Thiessen and her husband Bob we left the following day for Jim's home in Baltimore, Maryland.

Their final home was in Virginia to where they moved in 1973. Appropriately, they named their house *Tyntesfield*.

Robert Thiessen and Violet Summerell near Tyntesfield 1944 or 1945. (Tracey Brake – niece of Robert Thiessen)

In Winnie's story, she refers to Violet Summerell Thiessen. Violet Summerell, a local girl from Nailsea, was nineteen years old when the 74th arrived at Tyntesfield. Like many local girls, from time to time she went to the enlisted men's dances at the hospital. The band's piano player was Bob Thiessen, a twenty-seven year-old corporal who worked in the unit's administration section. As he played, Bob particularly noticed Violet on the dance floor so, during his next break from playing, he asked her to dance. She agreed, and their relationship developed.

Bob left Tyntesfield when the 74th transferred to mainland Europe but, over the next two years, he and Violet kept in touch by letter and Bob's occasional visits. On one of these visits, Bob asked Violet if she would marry him and she accepted his proposal. At the beginning of May 1947, Violet flew to New York's Idlewilde airport (now JFK) to be greeted by Bob, and for the next month she lived with Bob's parents. On 7 June 1947, they married at Bogota New Jersey and finally set up home in Bergenfield NJ.

Chapter Nine

Going Back Stateside – Repatriation Home

Following hospital treatment, some casualties recovered fully and returned to their units to resume duties; others did not recover sufficiently to return to their units and were allocated to lighter duties elsewhere; and some casualties never recovered to enable them to perform any form of army duty. A casualty not able to return to duty was customarily evacuated to the Unite States – in American wartime parlance, the 'Zone of the Interior' (ZI). A patient in the last category was judged to be unfit for further duty when:

- His injuries or medical condition required an extremely long convalescent period.
- Equipment or facilities in UK general hospitals were not available to treat his injuries.
- His injuries would result in his being medically discharged upon recovery.
- Men whose evacuation was deemed a military necessity [for security reasons?]
- And, generally, blinded patients, those with severe burns, face or jaw injuries, some grave orthopaedic patients and the hopelessly psychotic and mentally ill: all were classed as 'high priority' for repatriation.

Hospital medical officers determined the nature of surgical or medical care required by a wounded or sick casualty. In June 1942, General Hawley advocated a general evacuation policy, effective from August 1943, to deal with repatriation of the wounded. Basically, the policy stated that if a patient's medical or surgical needs including essential recuperation would exceed 180 days then he or she would be unfit to return to duty in the European Theatre of Operations and would be repatriated to the United States.

In the middle of October 1944, this policy was amended to 120 days and, in some instances, to ninety days or even less. This meant that if a patient admitted to a general hospital in the UK would, in the opinion of his doctors, be fit for duty within the number of days set out in the evacuation policy, he would be retained and treated, returned to his original unit or sent to a replacement centre when he had recovered. If, on the other hand, the patient's chances of recovering within that time were remote or non-existent, he or she would be sent to a hospital in the United States as soon as they could safely be moved so great a distance.

Between August 1942 and December 1943, 7,800 American patients returned to the United States. Of these, approximately 1,600 litter cases and mental patients returned on the few available British and Canadian hospital ships. Until the end of 1943, the US had no specifically equipped ships in which to transport wounded, and the first one to operate from the UK did not become available until just before D-Day. By March 1944, the need to repatriate injured patients increased significantly due to the expansion of American forces in the UK and the need to clear hospital beds in readiness to treat wounded following the D-Day landings. At this time, the threat to convoys from German U-boats had considerably reduced, so an increasing number of litter cases and ambulatory patients returned home on American troopships despite their not being able to display Geneva Convention symbols indicating that they were repatriating wounded. Other wounded returned to the States on fast liners like the *Queen Mary* and *Queen Elizabeth*.

From September 1942, some casualties returned by air to the States in C-54 *Skymaster* four-engined transport planes from the US Transatlantic Military Air Terminal at Prestwick, Scotland. By the end of 1943, only 116 patients, many of them ambulatory and in the 'high priority' category, returned by air. Into 1944, the carrying capacity of the C-54 was only

C-54 Skymaster in flight.

Interior view of C-54 Skymaster showing wounded on litters supported on steel frames.
(WW2 US Medical Research Centre: www.med-dept.com)

eighteen litter patients so, compared with sea-repatriated patients, the air route for this type of patient was not particularly efficient. From 1 January 1944 to 31 May 1944, only about 1,600 patients left Britain by plane.

As the land war intensified in the early months of 1945, an ever increasing number of American wounded awaited their turn to be repatriated, together with wounded Germans who would sit out the remaining months of the war in the US as POWs. All available American hospital ships and some British were loaded to capacity, departing mostly from Avonmouth and Liverpool, and turnaround times were kept to a minimum. The British 'Queen' liners, *Elizabeth* and *Mary*, and other liners in use were loaded to capacity on their return trips to the States departing mostly from the River Clyde ports near Glasgow, so more and more effort was directed at using the American C-54 transport aircraft despite its relatively low capacity.

Evacuation numbers generally now rapidly increased: 24,666 patients crossed the Atlantic by plane and ship in January 1945, another 29,743 went in February 1945, and 30,410 returned in March 1945. And with ever more C-54s being pressed into service, evacuation by air climbed to 2,000 patients per month.

Following its changed primary role to that of a holding hospital in December 1944, most of the 74th's patients after that time were held in the hospital awaiting transport back to the States. Many of these returned to the US on ships through Bristol's deep-water port at Avonmouth on the

River Severn. Only twelve miles from Tyntesfield by road, Avonmouth was ideally situated for returning patients to the US by sea. It had all the necessary portside facilities for handling wounded soldiers, and was also well located relative to most US hospitals in the south of England.

From mid-September 1944 onwards, twelve US hospital ships, designated USAHS [United States Army Hospital Ships], ferried wounded from Avonmouth to Charleston, South Carolina, in a total of twenty-two trips, the last departing on 17 June 1945. Most of the ships carried between 500 and 600 wounded, though one, the *Louis A Milne*, was exceptional. This ship with a crew of 145, carried 846 wounded, cared for by 259 medical personnel. It had six wards each with a sixty-eight-bed capacity, seven isolation wards with four beds in each, and two well-equipped operating rooms. On its trip departing Avonmouth on 22 May 1945, its Post Exchange (PX) sold 56,000 packs of cigarettes, 288 cigarette lighters, 33,000 candy bars, 4,500 razor blades and 2,520 packets of peanuts. In this same period, a number of British hospital ships assisted in transferring US wounded back to the States.

Although most of the 74th's patients returned to the US by sea, some returned by air. The majority of these travelled to Glasgow in hospital trains from Bristol Temple Meads station, thence on to Prestwick airfield by road, and finally to the States on the four-engined C-54 transport planes. And some made the trip directly to Prestwick from Filton airfield where, from D-Day onwards to the end of the war, many C-47 aircraft took off carrying wounded.

View towards Motor Pool. Building 47 in foreground right. A line of ambulances (left) prepare to take wounded to Bristol Temple Meads railway station. (Tracey Brake – niece of Robert Thiessen)

The story of Ed Souder, one of the wounded to be repatriated by way of the 74th GH and Avonmouth is typical. Edward L Souder was a Private First Class (PFC) in Company F, 405th Regiment, 102nd Infantry Division. Late in the afternoon of 28 November 1944, Ed was a passenger in a Jeep heading towards the town of Gerconsweiler, Germany, close to the Dutch border. A German 88mm shell exploded under the rear of the Jeep and shrapnel tore into his left buttock narrowly missing his spinal chord. He was taken to a field hospital in Holland, patched up and eventually evacuate by air to England, his journey ending three days after his wounding at the 102nd General Hospital near Devizes, Wiltshire. After four not wholly successful operations and with shrapnel still in him, Ed was declared unfit for further military duty and listed for return to the United States. Nearly four months after his wounding and now an ambulatory case, on Saturday 19 March 1945, Ed set out on the journey that would eventually see him back in the United States via the 74th. The following account is Ed's own words, though abridged to some extent, and with the author's comments for clarity, thus […]

Ed Souder photograph taken around 1944. (Ed Souder)

> *We boarded the bus slowly and at 1015 hours we rolled thru the gates of the 102nd Gen. Hosp., 4132 U.S. AHP [Army Hospital Plant], on our way to Bristol and the 74th General Evac. Hospital [sic]. We got there by noon the same day and were processed at the Hqtrs and sent up to ward 14 on top of the hill. Here we turned in our records, were assigned bunks and blankets and went down to lunch. We stayed here – had no work to do – just lived and ate and slept and played cards and watched the shipping numbers and names as the boys moved out – some before and after our arrival went first. Then our names were read on the 24th of March to be on the alert-ready list so for a week we lived close and signed out when we went down to the show. On Friday, the 30th, we were told that we would leave at noon the next day. So we got our bags ready, dressed nicely and ate chow early and were in the tent at the foot of the hill at 12:30. Here we waited for an hour and then we were given our tags and X-rays.*

Then we loaded in big buses and took off for a drive thru Bristol to the dock [Avonmouth] and our first sight of our ship. We all wanted to cheer but didn't as we got off the bus. Each man was helped by a darky [black soldier] who took our small personal belongings and put an arm around us and walked us into a covered shed. Here we were put in groups and handed a different colored tag. I got a red one with a blue edge. Then as our names and ASN [Army Service Number] were read we were assisted up the gangplank and down to our ward aft. Here we were assigned bunks and I got a lower one by a porthole. There we stayed until we were issued robes and PJs [pyjamas] and changed then a short time later we were given instructions, examined by the doctor, a Capt. Blair and allowed on deck for a while. Soon we cast off and started moving only to tie up further down the dock. We ate supper and before bedtime we each got a quart of milk and went to sleep at 2200. The next morning we got up and made our beds, then ate and at 0900 [31 March 1945] our ship the St. Mihiel cast off past the huge 1000-bed Wisteria and bound for the U.S.A., thank God! Our dream was now coming true. [The Wisteria in fact had a patient capacity of 601.]

It would be hard to set down all my thoughts as we went along in convoy past the first mine nets and slowly left the green cliffs of England under that cloudy sky. The water was quite rough and we did not stay on deck very long. By late afternoon we were leeward of an island [Lundy?] at the mouth of the estuary to wait for minesweepers to clear

US Army Hospital Ship St. Mihiel. (US Navy photograph – NARA)

126

our path as the high wind had broken some loose from their moorings. That night we played cards, read the books in our new blue and red Red Cross bags, drank milk, and got used to the life on ship – once again.

The next day was Easter Sunday, so I read my Easter story and looked at my pictures and went to sleep. The next morning (Sunday) we had fried ham for breakfast and then several of us went to Easter service on C deck. The ships Chaplin (sic) and a trio of nurses put on a nice little service and we even had an Easter lily on the altar, of which all seemed rather proud. And the waves kept banging against the porthole glass and the wind was very high. The ship rolled heavily from side to side and even with reduced speed we took water over the prow each time. The fellows up on A and B decks were lashed into their bunks and everyone went around by grabbing from one bedpost to the next. Easter evening I started to get seasick and ate some tablets for it. They were yellow and came in black paper and were bitter to the taste. So I kept pretty close to my bed the next day and after that it didn't bother me much.

The cyclone kept up for 3 days and the ship kept up just 2 knots an hour about 20 miles per day. The last night as we neared the Canary Islands the ship struck a huge wave and we listed 45 degrees. The ship capsizes at 57 degrees. I stayed in my bunk but on A and B decks there were 15 broken bones caused by that wave. God how we hated to see those men up there minus legs and arms, in steel and plaster body casts, stinking wounds, traction cases and then the ICE [?] over on C and D deck aft in the lock wards – guys like you and me – virtually maimed for life – think they would have been better off dead but I guess God wanted to let them suffer some more – and why was I spared?

Its crossing of the Atlantic finally over, the St Mihiel docked at Charleston, South Carolina, mid-morning on 15 April 1945, and Ed travelled on to Stark General Hospital for continuing treatment.

Chapter Ten

Leisure Time

Hospital orchestras

Both the 56th and 74th formed orchestras, drawing talented musicians from within their personnel. In the summer of 1943, while the 56th was still in the United States, a search for musical talent within the hospital staff uncovered sufficient numbers to form the 56th General Hospital Orchestra. First at home and then at Tyntesfield, the men of the ten-piece orchestra devoted many hours of their off-duty time to practice, and rapidly developed into an accomplished group. They provided the music for many parties and dances at the hospital, and were also in great demand by other American service organisations in the locality. At one typical engagement, held on 20 April 1944, the orchestra provided the musical entertainment for a dance at the village hall in Westbury, a suburb of Bristol. The dance was organised by the 22nd Mobile Reclamation & Repair Squadron that was based at the Bristol Aeroplane Company's airfield at Filton on the north side of Bristol. Here, in late November 1943, an area of the airfield had been made available to the USAAF, designated *Station 803*. The 22nd MR & RS recovered and repaired crashed American aircraft, and assembled new aircraft delivered in modules to Avonmouth docks.

How and when the 74th's fourteen-piece orchestra formed is not clear

74th GH – Parade at flag lowering ceremony – occasion unknown. (University of Tennessee)

56th GH band 'Doctors of Rhythm'. (Molly Placko)

56th GH band performing. (Molly Placko)

74th General Hospital band. (Tracey Brake – niece of Robert Thiessen)

from official records, but it is reasonable to assume that it too originated in the United States and its developing professionalism followed a similar path to that of the 56th's.

The brass section of the orchestras of both units also performed at formal retreat parades and other ceremonies held on the hospital parade ground. [The retreat ceremony signalled the end of the official duty day at which time the flag was lowered, and served also for paying respect to the flag. Originally it signified the requirement of sentries to challenge personnel until sunrise and for soldiers to return to their quarters.]

Patient recreation

As described earlier, the American Red Cross provided many leisure facilities in a converted ward building for the use of patients.

At Christmas 1943 with the 56th and in 1944 with the 74th, every effort was made to bring happiness to all in the hospital. The local estate woods yielded Christmas trees, holly and mistletoe; and patients and ward staff made paper streamers and acquired tinsel and other sparkly items to decorate every ward and personnel quarters. A number of patients, dressed as Santa Claus, handed out Red Cross presents to patients and staff. A party was held in the patients' recreation hall, also festively decorated for the occasion; local individuals joined the staff to entertain the patients with Christmas carols; and local civilian organisations provided flowers, presents and souvenirs. At Christmas 1944, a local singing group, the 'Merry Beggars', a mix of adults

74th GH – piano entertainment for three soldiers in enlisted men's club November 1944. (Dr. Sanders Marble)

74th GH – bed entertainment for wounded soldiers on 3 November 1944. (Dr. Sanders Marble)

74th GH – two soldiers playing drafts (US 'checkers') 4 November 1944. (Dr. Sanders Marble)

74th GH – soldier playing snooker in enlisted men's club 3 November 1944. (Dr. Sanders Marble)

and children sang carols through the wards of the 74th to bring cheer to the soldiers. The origin of the group's name appears now lost, but they neither begged nor were paid for their time; they sang solely to help make Christmas a happy time for the soldiers so far from home.

In addition to its fourteen-piece orchestra, the 74th formed a choir at Hoylake in March 1944. On Christmas Eve that year, it sang at a 10:00 am service, and at 8:00 pm performed what was termed in the programme a *Christmas Musical*. Some of the civilian staff at the hospital also attended the services. The programme stated:

> *The Chapel Choir now ranks as one of the best in the ETO [European Theatre of Operations] and it has been a major factor in the success of the Chapel services of the 74th General Hospital.*

Staff recreation

As originally built, the officers' and nurses' mess buildings each included an ante-room almost as large as the dining rooms. Lt Col Sheehan arranged for the officers' ante-room to be converted into a dining room, thereby combining the officers' and nurses' dining rooms in one building. The original nurses' dining room was converted into a recreation room and club for the use of all officers, both hospital personnel and patients. A separate clubroom was set up for enlisted men.

Although doctors, nurses and enlisted men worked long hours, they all looked forward to time away from their hospital duties. The clubrooms offered facilities for general relaxation where men and women could read, write letters home, listen to the radio, quietly reflect on life, and have a drink in the evenings. The club opened at five o'clock in the afternoon and closed promptly at ten o'clock every evening. Both clubrooms included a bar where staff could buy beers and soft drinks, and officers at their bar could also buy spirits, though strictly rationed each month. The enlisted men's bar, however, apparently offered beer and soft drinks only.

Benjamin Dangerfield III, who managed the 56th PX, recalls listening to the music 'Hit Parade and Command Performance' broadcast on the local Armed Forces stations relayed from America via short wave. And, on 4 July 1943, using equipment and studio facilities courtesy of the BBC, the Americans also began broadcasting news and music to troops in the UK through the AFN [American Forces Network]. This service kept them up to date with news from home. And the 'Stars and Stripes', the weekly-published American forces newspaper, was always available in the clubrooms.

Army regulations allowed relationships between male and female officers, but forbade relationships between enlisted men and nurses. More than 400 young and healthy enlisted men, the majority under thirty years

Officers & nurses club. (Molly Placko)

Another view of officers & nurses club. (Molly Placko)

56th GH Officers and nurses spirit drinks chit. The chit was punched to show that the allocated ration had been taken. (Molly Placko)

Officers and Nurses Club

56 TH **General Hospital**

U. S. Army.

No. 1845

old, worked in various departments throughout the hospital complex and most needed female companionship from time to time. Although many had girlfriends, sweethearts and wives at home, they all knew that the prospect of the war ending soon and their returning home was slim. Denied relationships with the female nurses in the hospital, the enlisted men had to look elsewhere for female company, in the local villages and towns and in Bristol. The local women, many with husbands and sweethearts scattered all over the world in the military services, likewise sought male companionship. Inevitably, therefore, natural urges took over and relationships and love affairs developed between enlisted men and local women, and probably between officers and local women.

Although not recorded in the official records of either of the hospital units, it is likely that some local women became pregnant by men from the hospital, and no doubt the commanding officers of both units would have had fathers of unfortunate daughters banging on his office door demanding that one of his men 'do right' by his daughter. Certainly, in the 298th General Hospital at Frenchay, this situation occurred and was generally dealt with by a chaplain and Red Cross social worker, often resulting in a 'happy' solution, though what 'happy' means can only be imagined. At Frenchay, the commanding officer often punished an enlisted man proved to have caused a pregnancy by reducing him to the lowest rank and consequent minimum salary.

For a nurse or Red Cross worker to become pregnant was viewed upon with unqualified disfavour by the army hierarchy. In strictly military terms, pregnancy would 'interfere with her dedication to duty in the war effort'. Again, no record can be found that pregnancy befell any nurse from either the 56th or 74th GHs, but army regulations of the time required a pregnant nurse to report the fact to her CO whereupon she was sent back to the United States before the end of the fifth month of her pregnancy. If she failed to report then her baby was delivered in the military hospital and she and the baby were then shipped back home.

Both the 56th and 74th units provided other opportunities in various forms for hospital personnel to 'let their hair down'. Weekly dances were held on base for enlisted men, with local girls being bussed in. And the officers also had their weekly dances, held on Saturday nights, though exclusively for officers and nurses.

Alice Boehret, a nurse with the 74th, recalled that most of the nurses wore evening dress to the dances '...so we could be human'. She said that some of the nurses felt uncomfortable, a little guilty perhaps, because male and female officers could have dates but enlisted soldiers could not date nurses. The strict adherence to rank protocol within the American Army applied off base also. She recalled that when her brother, also an army soldier, got leave from serving in France and visited her in Bristol, she had to carry a note in her pocketbook saying that *Lieutenant Alice C Boehret was allowed to be seen with Corporal Karl J Boehret*, 'in case we got stopped'.

The city of Bristol offered many diverse opportunities for off-base leisure time including theatres, cinemas, pubs, the American Red Cross Service Clubs and the 'ladies of pleasure'.

Ben Dangerfield recalls:

About once a week, groups of us [enlisted men] went into Bristol by army truck where we usually spent our time at the bar of the Prince's Hotel which the local girls liked.

Hospital staff, particularly the enlisted men, also visited the pubs closer to the hospital including the Failand Inn, the Angel in the nearby village of Long Ashton, the Battleaxes at Wraxall and the pubs in Nailsea. All were within a few miles of the hospital and no doubt would have afforded a pleasant walk in spring and summer. Many relationships between GIs and local families began in the pubs, with soldiers being invited to join in games of darts and cards, and often into the homes of local people. Many of these relationships continued after the war with exchanges of letters and sometimes visits by the GIs to the homes of those locals who had befriended them.

The majority of local pubs welcomed Americans despite their initial moans about English beer, albeit mostly humorously. Aside from its unfamiliar taste and generally low alcohol content, for the GI palette it was usually served too warm because few pubs had any refrigeration equipment. A common quip of the GI after tasting English beer was 'pour it back in the horse'.

The Angel was particularly popular with Ben Dangerfield and his half-dozen close friends, but they also visited other pubs nearby, sometimes on foot and at other times by bicycle. Ben recalls:

We called ourselves 'The Union' and partied on birthdays and any occasion, and on most nights would assemble at the nearby Angel pub to chat, sing and drink – and hope for the appearance of Scotch [whisky].

Sometimes we crossed the nearby fields at Tyntesfield on our way through blackouts to the Angel pub and trying to avoid what the cows left on our path.

Before their posting to Tyntesfield, the 56th knew they were to be one of the hospital units to transfer to France soon after D-Day to set up a general hospital closer to the fighting. On one of their visits to the Angel, Hank Kogan, a member of 'The Union' wrote a parody of the song 'Pistol Packin' Mama' titled 'Channel Hopping Daniel' [reference to Lt Col Daniel

Sheehan, the hospital commanding officer]. The original song 'Pistol Packin' Mama 'sung by Bing Crosby and The Andrews Sisters was a popular hit in America in January 1944. The verses of Hank's rendering went something like this:

We don't want to cross to France
In channel hopping tubs
We just want to chase the girls
And drink up all the pubs

Chorus

Lay that bedpan down babe
Lay that bedpan down
Channel hopping Daniel
Lay that bedpan down

We are pretty brave and true
Our arms and legs we love
We'd rather be hit by falling rain
Than bombs from up above

Chorus

Our only ambition in this war
Is to get home ahead of our tags
But if we follow Daniel
We all go home in bags

Chorus

Give him his chicken and make him stay
In England with the best
Let's not go to Europe
All we want is rest

Chorus

When the bullets start to fly
And we are killed in mass
Where will Col Sheehan be
Out on a two-day pass.

From time to time all the staff were able to obtain leave passes. In her report after the war's end, the 56th's chief nurse said:

> We were much in demand for parties at units stationed in the neighbourhood and once a month we had a 48-hour pass into London. Almost everyone had a 7-day leave during our stay in England – Scotland and the southern coast being the favorite vacation spots.

Alice Boehret's initial forebodings about little to do in off-duty time were perhaps premature. During her time at Tyntesfield, she frequently visited nearby Bristol and many of the cities and towns on today's sightseeing itinerary, including London, Bath, Cheltenham, Stratford-upon-Avon, nearby Weston-super-Mare and Scotland. She also experienced her first air flight in August 1944. In a letter home, she told a friend:

> On Saturday [5 August 1944] we had the grandest time. We went to an aircorps dance over 160 miles away. We had to go by plane. It was wonderful. Now I know why people insist on flying. The dance itself wasn't so hot but the transportation!!! 'Mag the Bag' [chief nurse Margaret Hornickel] doesn't know about this little jaunt. I hope we can go again, just for the ride.

Many of the men, both officers and enlisted men, also took part in on-base athletics pastimes. Baseball, volleyball and boxing matches were popular

74th GH – Enlisted men of playing volleyball. (University of Tennessee)

though whether officers boxed against enlisted men is not recorded.

In the summer and autumn months of 1944, with the 74th running the hospital, bicycle rides around lanes in nearby countryside were very popular with all ranks. The nurses, particularly, enjoyed stopping off in a farmer's field to have a picnic, rounding off the day with a visit to one of the local pubs.

Venereal disease

An almost inevitable outcome of soldiers' recreation and associating with local 'ladies of pleasure' or 'easy women' was the possibility of picking up – in today's terminology – *sexually transmitted diseases,* but in wartime simply called VD. In 1940, the US government published recommendations for soldiers in a pamphlet titled 'Sex Hygiene and Venereal Disease'.

Among its pieces of bizarre advice and gloomy warnings were: 'Most prostitutes have venereal disease'; 'It is not necessary to have sexual intercourse in order to keep strong and well'; and 'A healthy body and a healthy mind lead to happiness'. But, recognising that men are fallible, the pamphlet also advised: 'If you do not have self-control then do not fail to take safety measures'.

Venereal disease, universally known as VD, cost the army heavily in time lost from duty and diversion of medical resources as well as being a source of political and social tension between American and British people. All troops were shown films about limiting or avoiding catching VD, and many posters, often prepared by enlisted men, were prominently displayed throughout the hospital presenting the same warnings. All channels of communication urged men to avoid illicit sexual contact on grounds of patriotism, unit pride, faithfulness to loved ones at home, and personal self-interest, emphasising that it invariably led to infection.

The 56th appointed a 'Venereal Disease Control Officer' who, together with the chaplains, regularly pleaded with soldiers during formal talks and lectures to abstain from sexual contact. But, if unable to abstain, then all were urged to use condoms, provided free by the army to all men at a rate of six per man per month. One of the first notices to be posted on the 56th's bulletin boards stated in rather formal terminology:

> *Mechanical prophylaxis materials are available at the hospital post exchange, [PX] without cost.*

But, in truth, all appeals to GIs to abstain were unrealistic and often went unheeded. Most men were under thirty years old, physically fit, a long way from home and lonely.

During its time at Tyntesfield, the 56th dealt with sixty cases of VD –

syphilis and gonorrhea – mostly using sulpha drugs. At the time, penicillin, the new 'wonder' drug, was in short supply and was used only where customary treatments failed.

Chapter Eleven

Food, Laundry and Waste

In the early days of the American servicemen's presence in the UK, the food generally available to them was what the British ate, not what they were used to, and they were most unhappy. Prior to the start of WWII, the United Kingdom imported huge quantities of food including more than fifty per cent of its meat, seventy per cent of its cheese and sugar, nearly eighty per cent of fruits and about seventy per cent of cereals and fats. Unsurprisingly, a principal strategy of the German Navy was to prevent ships carrying food arriving in the UK, with the intention of starving the nation into submission. Acknowledging the German Navy's intent, the British Government introduced rationing of certain foods early in 1940. This included bacon, butter, sugar, meat, tea, jam, biscuits, breakfast cereals, cheese, eggs, milk and canned fruit. Home-grown vegetables, however, were mostly readily available, particularly potatoes.

The American authorities knew that feeding its service personnel with good food was essential to maintaining high morale. They quickly appreciated that British rations threatened morale and even efficiency among their servicemen and women. So they promptly found space in the holds of ships crossing the Atlantic to the UK for foods that their people were more accustomed to. By the end of the summer of 1942, Americans in the UK were eating 'American' foods.

Some fruits like grapefruit, bananas, grapes and melons were not imported for UK citizens' consumption for the whole war period. Oranges, however, were occasionally available in the UK though generally only for children and pregnant women. To the American soldier, however, oranges were generally plentiful, and they generously passed them on to British families, particularly to the children. Home-grown fruits like apples and pears were available, but only for short periods when in season.

And, for hospital patients, the Quartermaster Corps insisted that:

> *Food service at hospitals must be the finest possible. Sick and injured soldiers deserve only the best.*

Since the hospital was a fixed installation, the food provided was classed as the

A-ration, a term used in the United States Armed Forces for a meal provided to troops that was prepared using fresh, refrigerated or frozen foods. The aim, though not always achieved, was to provide at least seventy per cent fresh food. A trained dietician on the hospital staff constructed standard recipes with emphasis on nutrients, palatability and attractiveness; and planned daily menus with special reference to proper diet and nutritional balance using the best available food supplies.

When the hospital first opened, the 56th operated four messes: one for officers, one for nurses, one for enlisted men and a fourth for ambulatory patients. These occupied two buildings and were attached to their separate cookhouses, food being served using the cafeteria-style of service. Those patients who were handicapped by casts etc were served at their tables by enlisted men. Patients confined to bed were provided with meals in their wards. For bed patients, food was conveyed from the cookhouses to the wards in carts. The carts incorporated tanks that were filled with hot water at the cookhouse to keep the food hot in transit and, on arrival at the wards, food was reheated as necessary in the ward kitchen before being served to patients.

In his report covering their time at Tyntesfield, Lt Col Daniel S Sheehan, the 56th's commanding officer, said about the food:

> The ration is found to be good and varied, with nutrient values sufficient for all dietary requirements. The ration is thought to be comparable with the issue ration in the United States in most respects. While fresh vegetables of root and cabbage variety were more prominent in the menus during the winter months of 1943 than personnel had previously been accustomed to, this detracted neither from wholesomeness or food values.

In the last sentence, is he politely trying to disguise a reference to the one vegetable widely grown in the UK in winter months but almost universally loathed by Americans – the sprout? A perhaps tongue-in-cheek anecdote from the time is that the commanding officer of an American bomber base in East Anglia ordered his pilots that, if they had to crash-land in England, they were to make sure it was in a field of sprouts!

But even the Americans could not import fresh milk and eggs, foodstuffs that did not travel well, and missed terribly by the GIs. These items were rationed to UK citizens, generally one egg per week and milk sometimes as little as two pints per week per person. But, in the countryside particularly, the black market was a thriving industry. In exchange for some of the luxury food items available to the Americans that the local people had not seen for years, eggs and milk often found their way into the hospital kitchens. Dehydrated eggs in powdered form, however, was widely produced in America and Canada and shipped to the UK to supplement the egg ration both for civilians and Americans alike. Many ingenious recipes were devised to make the powdered egg more palatable; nonetheless it was no substitute for the real thing.

Colonel Teperson, the 74th GH's commanding officer wryly observed:

Powdered eggs have been a constant challenge to the cooks.

A Red Cross worker with the 188th General Hospital at Cirencester, Gloucestershire, commented that delaying getting up in the mornings until 6:30 to start work at 7:00 enabled her to miss the powdered eggs in the mess, and also gave her extra time in bed. Very likely many at Tyntesfield adopted the same routine.

One of the few foods not rationed in the UK during wartime was fish and chips, though obtainable at an inflated price. The British Government contended that, if fisherman were prepared to put to sea to catch fish and face enemy submarines, then they could quite reasonably charge a premium for the fish they caught. And, despite the premium, the availability of fish led to a rapid increase in the consumption of fish and chips – the potatoes for chipping being readily available. Restaurants reported record numbers of customers and fish and chip shops started opening during the day to meet the demand. Whether this dish was ever cooked in the kitchens of the 56th and 74th is not known, but certainly some Americans enjoyed the meal from Bristol's 'takeaways'.

The hospital kitchens included the potato in various guises on most of its menus. Peeling the large quantities of potatoes needed for 1,500 or more people usually fell to the enlisted men of the hospital units, and this task was usually referred to as *KP* duties.

KP duty – kitchen police or kitchen patrol – was a term applied to enlisted men assigned to work on kitchen duties, but excluded food cooking. The term probably derives from US military usage where the word 'police' is used as a verb to mean 'to clean' or 'keep in order'. KP, therefore, could be either the work or the personnel assigned to perform such work. KP duties included any tedious task associated with food: peeling potatoes and preparing vegetables, washing dishes and scrubbing pots and pans, sweeping and mopping kitchen and mess floors, wiping tables, serving food, and any other job kitchen staff could dream up and decided to dole out. Originally, KP duty was assigned to military men who had committed a minor offence or breach of discipline while on military service, but not warranting severe punishment. Often, however, it was a duty of necessity; an enlisted man's name was put on a rotating list and, when his name came up, he was put on KP duty. The British nearest equivalent of the term was 'jankers'.

But despite the range of foods enjoyed by the hospital staff and patients, mostly unavailable luxuries to the general public, certain foods and other items were scarce. While the hospital PX stocked many items, many desired items could be obtained only in parcels sent by relatives and friends back home in the States.

Alice Boehret often wrote to her mother and friends asking for things to be sent over from the States. Extracts from a letter to her sister Dorothy in May 1944 illustrates the sorts of desirables not readily available from the PX:

74th GH – 'KP' duty peeling potatoes.
(University of Tennessee)

We are about to have hot tea and hot soup. Kay Wall – in the bed next to me – got three boxes today, with everything in them from soup to nuts. And I mean that! It was a dehydrated soup and there was a jar of peanuts. For the rest of the box – cheese and pickles, olives, tea, coffee, candy and toilet paper. We had such terrible toilet paper in the billets. Each sheet says 'Government Property'. How do you like that!

Another regular plea of Alice to her mother and friends was for hairnets. For a nurse with long hair, as Alice had, keeping it up and tidy was vital and this could best be achieved using a hairnet. These, it would seem, were in short supply in the UK in 1944. Another item in short supply, but so required by hospital staff thousands of miles from home, was writing paper. Alice repeatedly asked for sheets of plain writing paper to be included with letters and parcels from home.

Laundry

Two companies in local towns provided a laundry service for both the 56th and 74th GHs. The 56th GH laundry was taken for cleaning twice a week by hospital personnel and exchanged for clean linen on the same trip. The 74th used the same local laundries but, since they had many more patients than the 56th, they needed to take soiled laundry for cleaning on three days each week – Monday, Wednesday and Friday. When the 74th was at its busiest, 18,000 to 21,000 items per week needed cleaning. The commanding officers of both hospital units praised the local laundries for their excellent service.

Enlisted personnel similarly had their laundry done under contract by the two local laundries, with every person limited to nine pieces weekly. However, with the high demand for cleaning hospital laundry and also providing a service to other army bases in the area, the laundries were often overwhelmed by volume, so enlisted personnel laundry was often up to a week late being returned. Officers and nurses also used nearby private laundries, but by personal arrangement rather than by hospital contract. Most of the nurses, however, washed their underclothes themselves and hung them to dry on lines erected in their huts.

Waste

With many food items either rationed or unavailable in Britain, hospital staff, in deference to its hosts, paid great attention to minimising food waste, the CO of the 74th, particularly, being a devotee of the principle. As in British homes throughout the war, the hospital saved potato and vegetable peelings, unused or leftover vegetables and meat from the tables in the so-called *pig bins*. The local council regularly collected the bins, sterilised and processed the food waste, and sold to it to farmers to feed to their pigs.

At the end of 1944 and into the first few months of 1945, the daily patient census averaged around the 1,100 mark and, with 611 staff also based in the hospital, it generated a huge amount of waste material. Used wound dressings and other 'soft' hospital waste, possibly including much paper, were burned in the hospital incinerator. Although this process reduced material bulk, the residue, also including discarded plaster casts, still had to be disposed of somewhere. Conveniently for the hospital, Long Ashton Rural District Council, the local administrative authority, made available two disused quarries for hospital use:

Typical WWII poster urging people to save kitchen waste for feeding pigs.

one on the nearby Failand Golf Course [now Bristol & Clifton Golf Club] and the other at Christchurch on the outskirts of the town of Clevedon; and these proved adequate for the hospital needs. Before the Americans left Tyntesfield, they tidied both quarries and capped them with topsoil, to the satisfaction of the health inspector.

Chapter Twelve

Transit Camp on Watercatch

When the Allied armies landed on the beaches of Normandy on 6 June 1944, 1.7 million American servicemen and women were based in the United Kingdom. In the weeks leading up to D-Day, 130,000 men left their training bases and moved into tented camps in marshalling areas near to the ports of embarkation in the counties of Cornwall, Devon, Dorset and Hampshire in readiness for the channel crossing. Following the initial landings on the beaches, codenamed Utah and Omaha, over the next ninety days the Americans planned to move another 1.2 million men across the English Channel to reinforce the initial assault force. Thereafter, additional units as needed would continue to cross to France by sea for an indefinite period.

The ninety-five marshalling camps could accommodate 187,000 troops and 28,000 vehicles, so transfer of troops and equipment from their training camps to the marshalling areas in readiness for the channel crossing had to be carefully managed. In the first six months of 1944 to the week before D-Day, the number of American forces personnel in the UK rose from 774,000 to 1.537 million, with 217,000 new arrivals in the month of May alone. Existing facilities could not accommodate this huge increase. Moreover, many other units, airfield construction engineers for example, having completed their work in the UK and awaiting orders to transfer to France as part of the second phase of the invasion, had to be temporarily housed.

To accommodate these additional troops, their equipment and vehicles, many temporary camps were constructed in the south of England in the first half of 1944, known generally as 'transit' or 'in-transit' camps. These provided fairly basic facilities: sleeping accommodation mostly in tents, with other facilities – bathing, messing, administration, etc – often provided in tents but sometimes in more substantial buildings. These camps could accommodate units for a few days or months if necessary. One of these 'transit' camps was built on the north edge of the Tyntesfield Estate adjacent to the Clevedon-Failand road on what was known as the *Watercatch* field.

By May 1944, approximately eighty per cent of all American servicemen and women entered the United Kingdom by ship at ports on the rivers Clyde and Mersey. They crossed the Atlantic mostly in converted peacetime cruise liners, the crossing rarely taking more than about seven days. Seventy per cent of their equipment and other supplies, however, crossed the Atlantic mostly in comparatively slow convoys to the Bristol Channel ports, mainly Swansea, Cardiff, Newport and Avonmouth; and to the Mersey ports of Liverpool, Garston, Manchester and Birkenhead; these crossings often taking up to fifteen days.

The Americans aimed to ship army units' stores, vehicles and equipment to the United Kingdom in advance of its personnel, so that the two could be reunited as soon as possible after arriving. In practice, however, this aspiration was rarely achieved because of transportation and sailing delays in the United States, losses at sea due to enemy action, the inability of UK ports to cope with the number of ships to be unloaded, and the shortcomings of the beleaguered UK rail and road systems in moving materials and equipment to their correct destinations.

Although all personnel of military units aimed to depart the US together, this was not always achieved. So, the 'transit' camp provided an ideal temporary base where a unit could establish itself, assemble its complement of officers and enlisted men, and await delivery of its vehicles, equipment and stores. Meanwhile, in preparation for movement to France to join the battle, men continued their training in the transit camps, both physical and technical, before finally moving on to camps in marshalling areas near to their embarkation ports.

The Camp

Prior to the spring of 1944, the Watercatch field was just another peaceful meadow on which cows grazed. Then, in early March, the US *398* Engineer General Service Regiment (coloured), 2 Battalion, Company F moved onto the land with their bulldozers, cranes, concrete mixers and other equipment to construct another camp for American soldiers.

The 398th formed on 22 March 1943 at Camp Claiborne, Louisiana. In preparation for overseas movement, on 20 July 1943, the unit transferred to *Camp Shanks*, the principal staging camps for the port of embarkation (POE) at New York. On 25 July 1943, the unit set sail from pier 90 on the *Queen Mary*, and five days later, on 30 July, dropped anchor in the river off Greenock, Scotland. On 1 August, the unit's personnel finally boarded a train at Glasgow to travel to Devizes in the county of Wiltshire. From Devizes railway station, the men marched to their first base in England at Le Marchant, one mile west of Devizes. Over the next six days, the unit came together and took delivery of most of its equipment.

The regiment's first construction project was at Braunton, Devon to where it relocated on 7 August 1943. During the remaining months of the year to the end of December, they constructed a number of camps around the south-west and west of England, and Wales. They enlarged the 1,000-

man hutted camp at Brockley Combe, ten miles northeast of Weston-super-Mare and five miles from Tyntesfield, by erecting tents for 500 additional men; and improved the kitchen, shower and latrine facilities in the hutted areas of the camp. They modernised plumbing and electrical installations at twenty requisitioned houses in Weston-super-Mare; and enhanced and enlarged other existing camps at Burnham on Sea, Street and Glastonbury by erecting additional Nissen huts and installing plumbing, electrical and sewerage facilities.

According to the unit's official history: 'By March 16 1944, Headquarters had moved to a new location nine miles northwest of Taunton' in the grounds of Hestercombe House, Somerset.

Although the unit's Company F arrival date at Tyntesfield to start work on building the camp is not recorded in the unit's official history, it does state under a heading 'Operations completed by 15 April 1944':

> *Tyntesfield Camp at Failand consisted of constructing a 1,500-man tented camp with 17 Nissen and MOWP [Ministry of War Production] huts, water tower and distribution system, and electrical distribution. Paths covered 30,360 sq. ft.; hardstandings 59,500 sq. ft.; and 2500 lineal feet of 12-foot road.*

No records can be located detailing how many Nissen huts and MOWP buildings made up the total of seventeen erected, nor the use to which they were put. However, they would likely have included administration and records offices, toilet and ablution facilities, guardroom, kitchens and mess halls, general workshops, vehicle maintenance workshops, dispensary and first aid building, PX, classrooms and miscellaneous others. Toilets and ablutions, kitchens and mess halls, and administration and records offices

Typical WWII Nissen huts. (Martin Collins)

would likely have been housed in timber-framed MOWP buildings whereas workshops, PX and classrooms would probably have been in Nissen huts. Officers may have slept in Nissen huts, and enlisted soldiers certainly in tents, either the six-man pyramidal model or the later-introduced twelve-man M1942 Squad Tent. The MOWP buildings would have been similar to those used for hospital personnel sleeping quarters.

Having completed the Tyntesfield camp, Company F moved on to construct another camp nearby on the Failand Golf Course [now Bristol & Clifton Golf Club]. The company's official history shows that this also was a 1,500-man tented camp, similar to that at Tyntesfield, with seventeen Nissen and MOWP huts, water tower and distribution system, and electrical installations. Paths covered 38,400 sq ft; hardstandings 52,500 sq ft; and 2,100 lineal feet of twelve-foot road. Company 'F' of the 398th is known to have been based at Tyntesfield on 30 April 1944, so quite possibly the men lived in the camp while constructing the Failand camp.

Sometime during the following four weeks, the 398th departed Tyntesfield for Porthcawl in Glamorgan, South Wales, where it began extensive training in port construction and repair work in preparation for its deployment on mainland Europe.

Units at Tyntesfield

A full list of American units that stopped over at Tyntesfield's transit camp cannot be located. However, the following are known to have been in residence on the given dates though their arrival and departure dates are not always known:

31 May 1944
2 Mobile Radio Broadcasting Company
202 Quartermaster Battalion (M), HQ
457 Ordnance Evacuation Company
482 Ordnance Evacuation Company
602 Engineer Camouflage Battalion (Aviation) HQ
827 Engineer Aviation Battalion, Headquarters
3905 Quartermaster Truck Company
3907 Quartermaster Truck Company

30 June 1944
2 Mobile Radio Broadcasting Company
72 Public Service Battalion, 1 Service Team
482 Ordnance Evacuation Company
602 Engineer Camouflage Battalion (Army) HQ

5/12 July 1944
475th Military Police Escort Guard Company

Little is known about most of the units listed and the precise roles they played in WWII, and why they stayed over at Tyntesfield, but the records of a few of them have been located.

2nd Mobile Radio Broadcasting Company

The 2nd MRBC, together with others fulfilling similar roles, provided a vital yet little publicised service in Europe following the D-Day landings: it waged a psychological war against the enemy. Its primary mission was to crush the fighting morale of the enemy, both in their homes and at the front, and to sustain the morale of friendly populations in enemy-held territory. Its secondary mission was to provide information to the population in liberated areas to assist the appropriate military authorities to restore and then to maintain order.

Following its arrival in France, one of the unit's early tasks was to interrogate captured German soldiers to learn whatever it could about their units: deployment, psychology, feelings about the war, and anything else they considered useful. The scriptwriters, printers and broadcasters then prepared leaflets and broadcasts making use of the information they had gained from the interrogations. The aim was to persuade the Germans that continuing to fight was a total waste of time, and that they would be far better off to surrender.

The leaflets and broadcasts emphasised to the Germans that what the Allies had to say was not propaganda, but was simply giving them the factual state of the war that they were losing. They named towns that had been captured or encircled by the British, Americans and Russians. They highlighted the Allied superiority in men and materials: 'Look up to the sky and see the Allied bombers and fighters flying over your heads, unharried by German fighters, on their way to bomb your homes and families.'

The scriptwriters and broadcasters highlighted Germany's military disasters; they exposed the false promises of the Nazi party leaders and their selfishness and greed, contrasting the privileges they enjoyed with those of ordinary Germans. They repeatedly emphasized the hopelessness of the German cause and that surrender was not dishonourable, reassuring the soldier that he would be treated well and with respect by Allied armies, with strict adherence to the terms of the Geneva Convention.

The company produced tens of millions of leaflets in various forms in German, Polish, Russian and French languages. These were mainly delivered using purpose-designed artillery shells and aerial bombs. Broadcasts to the Germans urging them to surrender were made using mobile equipment mounted on various types of vehicles, often driven to within a few miles of the German lines. The company also produced and delivered newspapers for German soldiers and civilians, and broadcast radio programmes to the people of Europe from more permanent stations at Cherbourg, Rennes, Lorient and Luxembourg.

The 2nd MRBC was activated on 29 December 1943 at Camp Ritchie, Maryland. On 2 February 1944, it moved to the Psychological Training Centre at Camp Sharpe, Pennsylvania, where it recruited various specialists to prepare and write leaflets, newspapers, radio broadcast scripts and radio shows in French and German. Among others, it also numbered radio specialists, engineers to erect antenna towers, and printers.

The unit left Camp Sharpe on 20 March 1944 arriving at Camp Shanks, New Jersey, the port-of-embarkation camp for New York harbour. On 31 March, the unit, comprising 144 enlisted men and twenty officers, left Camp Shanks by train to travel the twenty-five miles to the pier in New York. They, and about 15,000 other soldiers, boarded the British liner *Queen Elizabeth* to a send-off by an army band and the customary coffee and doughnuts provided by American Red Cross girls. At 1:30 pm on 1 April 1944, the ship swung its broad hull into the narrows of the Hudson River and headed downstream on its way to England. After many U-boat scares and changes of course, the ship reached Gourock, Scotland in 6½ days, one more than the usual 5½ days.

Immediately after disembarking, the unit boarded a train for the 315-mile trip to the village of Charfield, in the county of Gloucestershire. After arriving at Charfield railway station, the unit travelled by road to its first tented camp at Synwell's playing field on a hill overlooking the town of Wotton-under-Edge, Gloucestershire. Over the next week or so, they engaged in physical fitness training, and in the evenings attended dances in the town and visited private homes. They also played a football match against the local town team, losing 3-2.

On 15 April 1944, all personnel left Wotton by road bound for Clevedon, in the county of Somerset, where the unit was assigned to the Psychological Warfare Branch, P&PW (Publicity and Psychological Warfare) Detachment, 12th Army Group of the US First Army. Initially, personnel were accommodated in houses in the centre of the town. Having settled in to their new posting, they attended various lectures on all aspects of their work, the political situation in Germany and the reasons for the war. They also engaged in morning callisthenics helping to keep everyone in good physical condition.

Meanwhile their equipment that had been shipped from Camp Sharpe on much slower convoys began to arrive. Now able to start proper training with their special equipment, the company left Clevedon on 6 May 1944 to move the few miles to the newly built camp on the Tyntesfield estate. Here they settled in and awaited the order to transfer to south coast embarkation camps in readiness for the move to France.

Training for all the disciplines in the unit in various forms now began in earnest. In their Tyntesfield camp, the men conducted exercises that included erecting a radio tower, setting up fixed radio stations, and testing mobile radio transmitters. They carried out further testing and tuning of their mobile transmitters by travelling away from Tyntesfield and playing back records to the receivers at camp. Meanwhile, members of the artillery section travelled to London to study the techniques for preparing leaflets for artillery shell delivery.

Immediately following the D-Day landings, items of equipment continued to arrive in a steady stream and the camp at Tyntesfield took on the appearance of a combat staging area. The radio broadcast section assembled four loudspeaker units mounted on 1½-ton trucks, and the printers finally acquired their vans and printing presses. Enlisted men waterproofed their Jeeps and fitted them with vertically extending exhaust stacks so that, if necessary, they could run from LSTs through shallow water and onto the landing beaches. Although the company strength varied – at one time there were 215 enlisted men and thirty-one officers – in the weeks before D-Day some left on special assignments with advance parties so that, just before the unit left Tyntesfield, the complement had reduced to 165 men and twenty-nine officers.

Finally, at noon on 20 June, in a sixty-vehicle convoy, the company left Tyntesfield and arrived at Hillingsbury, Hampshire after a journey of 110 miles. During the night of 23 June, personnel boarded LST-421 but

Jeep fitted with waterproofed engine compartment and snorkel. (George Morley)

remained at anchor off the coast for two days before moving out on the morning of 25 June for the journey across the channel. It landed on Omaha beach, on the French Normandy coast at 2:00 pm the next day.

475th Military Police Escort Guard Company

The following is extracted from a website set up and written by Private 1st Class Gene Herbener who served with the unit, telling the story of the 475th Military Police Escort Guard Company in Europe in WW2:

On Monday afternoon 19 June 1944, at 2:30 pm, all personnel of the 475th MPEG Co. boarded a troop train at Fort Custer, Michigan. Twenty-six hours later they arrived at Camp Shanks, New York. Camp Shanks was upriver from New York City in a sylvan glade above Nyack on the west bank of the Hudson. It was under the command of the Transportation Corps and was a jumping off point for troops embarking to the European Theater of Operations (ETO). At 13:00 on Friday, 23 June, the 475th boarded a river steamer, a harbour boat, and set sail for New York City. At 19:00 the company disembarked at Pier 86 and boarded ship NY-825, H.M.S. Eastern Prince. The cruise stateroom on this English freighter masquerading as a troop ship was in a forward hold defined as an "upper 'tween."

At 11:00 pm on Tuesday, 4 July 1944, the Eastern Prince anchored in the Firth of Clyde off Greenock, Scotland. Although the hour neared midnight, it was still bright daylight due to the northern latitude and double Daylight Saving Time (European War Time). Next day at about 3:30 pm, the 475th MPEG Co. was ferried ashore by harbour steamer. It entrained about an hour later on the L.M.S. Railway and left for the southern reaches of the U.K. Next morning, at 6:00 am, the train arrived in Bristol, England. The company was trucked about six miles to Tyntesfield Camp, APO #508 [American Post Office] near the village of Failand.

Gene recorded in his diary:

Friday, 7 July 1944
I have arrived safely in England or at least that's what I thought. But after trying to barter for a glass of cider and a pint of bitter in a pub [probably 'The Failand Inn'] down the hard road apiece last evening, I don't know how safely I have arrived. The 'coin of the realm' produces a minor brainstorm when one starts making purchases and the ha'pennies, pennies, threepences, sixpences and shillings start rolling.

Sunday, 9 July 1944
I sit here on my cot shivering in a brisk English wind that penetrates everything…
I enjoyed walking through the wooded country lanes, along neatly clipped
hedge. All seemed so peaceful, except there were no cars, just natives buzzing
by on their 'lanky, lean looking' bicycles (if bicycles might be described as such).

On Wednesday 12 July 1944, the 475th MPEG Co boarded a train in Bristol, England, at 10:30 am, and it arrived at the Knowlesy Street station in Bury, Lancashire (north of Manchester) at 5:00 pm.

No documents can be located listing American units having been stationed at the Tyntesfield transit camp following the departure of the 475th MPEG Co on 12 July 1944. However, at the adjacent camp on the Failand Golf course, the 1308 Signal Pigeon Company (Aviation) [communications unit] was in residence until 22 September 1944, and although this appears to be the last use of transit camps in the area, it is quite possible that other units spent short periods at Tyntesfield around this time.

The 74th GH may also have used some of the buildings after its use as a transit camp ended, but no evidence can be found to support this possibility. The camp certainly remained under military authority for some time after the 74th General Hospital departed on 26 June 1945, but its precise use and occupancy cannot be traced covering the twelve months or so following the 74th's departure.

Post War

Within about a three-mile radius of the Tyntesfield transit camp, other military camps were in use during WWII including at least one prisoner-of-war (POW) camp. All of these camps included varying numbers of Nissen huts and MOWP buildings.

An item in the minutes of Long Ashton Rural District Council dated 17 September 1946 under the heading 'Occupation of Service Camps – Squatters' refers to a communication to the council from the Ministry of Health in respect of some camps within the council's jurisdiction that had been declared surplus to requirements of government departments. Included in the list of camps offered to LARDC was 'Tyntesfield Camp' (Failand).

The minutes of another LARDC meeting dated 20 September 1946 refers to 'Tyntesfield – Failand Camp'. It reported that two families were known to be squatting in this camp but the Ministry of Health had decided that the buildings were totally unsuitable for housing purposes, so the council decided not to take on responsibility for this camp. The council asked the MOW to take necessary measures to prevent further unauthorised occupation of this camp.

At the same meeting, the council resolved that camps suitable for temporary housing accommodation were: Abbots Leigh, Martcombe camp

154

at Easton-in-Gordano (ex-POW), St George Wharf at Easton-in-Gordano and Weston Lodge at Redcliffe Bay. At these camps, squatters were already in occupation, and the council resolved to try to improve conditions to allow them to stay there. At the Abbots Leigh camp, twenty-six families (eighty-seven persons) were squatting; at Martcombe at Easton-in-Gordano, twenty-seven families (ninety-one persons); at St George's seven families (thirty persons); and at Weston Lodge camp (Redcliffe Bay) thirteen families (forty persons). It was decided that none of the buildings at these camps were suitable for conversion for five or ten years' occupancy. It regarded them as suitable only for very temporary accommodation, requiring first-aid repairs, provision of essential services, and minor adaptations.

Of the MOWP buildings that were to be improved, most were not divided into rooms, and LARDC agreed to supply the occupants with materials with which they could construct partitions to form two rooms for living and sleeping quarters. Most of the occupiers were willing to undertake this work. The minutes record that the council proposed to dismantle a few plasterboard huts [MOWP buildings] at Tyntesfield to obtain the necessary materials. Although not specifically stated in LARDC minutes, it seems likely that Nissen huts would not have been considered suitable for accommodation, and that these would probably have been used as stores, workshops, etc.

No information can be found to date Tyntesfield's transit camp's demolition. Today all that remains to show that the camp ever existed are the concrete floors of some of the buildings.

Typical WWII MOWP building. (Martin Collins)

Chapter Thirteen

The 56th GH After Tyntesfield

Hoylake Cheshire 14 May 1944 to 13 July 1944

Because the unit transferred to Hoylake for further training and not to run a hospital, no single base existed; therefore, personnel quarters were scattered. The requisitioned Stanley Hotel accommodated the unit's headquarters on the second floor, with officers' and nurses' messes on the ground floor. Two requisitioned buildings nearby housed the enlisted men's mess and other hospital departments. Two other nearby requisitioned buildings provided quarters for all officers; nurses and other females of the unit, like those of the 74th before them, lived with families in their own homes. Private homes also provided lodgings for forty per cent of the enlisted men, and eight requisitioned houses provided lodgings for the remainder. Officers and all female personnel bathed in bathrooms in the buildings where they slept, while enlisted men made use of Hoylake's public baths.

Hoylake Stanley Hotel. (Winston Hawkins)

Immediately after settling into their new surroundings, all personnel commenced intensive training including the routine close-order marching, callisthenics, military discipline and courtesy. In addition, they were taught how to do many new things: put on gas masks, pitch large heavy tents, erect light shelter tents, carry a wounded soldier on a litter, map read, and identify aircraft. They received instructions about vermin control, personal hygiene in insanitary conditions, conservation of supplies and equipment, and many other subjects that would make their lives and those of their patients tolerable in alien conditions.

The civilian population often turned out to 'see what the Yanks are up to now'. They would look on amused and fascinated as the Yanks marched along the roads wearing gas masks. When the organisation left town on an overnight route march and to bivouac, the oft-heard comment from locals was 'the Yanks have gone on a picnic again'.

From the war's-end nurses' report:

> *Here we concentrated on field training – wore fatigues [one/two piece work-day clothes] all day long, were billeted in English homes which required patience and considerable adjustment on the part of the nurses. It was the first time in over a year that we had private rooms; however, we all preferred our huts to this. Here movies were the main entertainment – most of us were so tired after classes that we wrote a letter and went to bed.*
>
> *Only too well do all of us remember the second day in Hoylake when we marched five miles in a downpour of rain and the terrific wind. We dropped into bed after the last class – 8 pm – completely exhausted, realising that hospital work had been pretty soft.*
>
> *We played softball and volleyball, we stood retreat, we drilled, we had four to six hours of classes every day and never in the same place – so we marched from place to place, and of course we tested the gas chamber again. We learned about booby traps, camouflage and a million other things all we combat soldiers must know. The final test was when we grabbed our bed-rolls, marched ten miles and pitched our pup tents [two-person ridge tent] for 24 hours as experience in the field.*

Then, on 13 May 1944, Lt Col Sheehan received an alert that the unit must be available for overseas movement any time after 25 May. Not wanting to be caught on the hop when the order to move eventually came, personnel immediately started checking that they had all the equipment they would need and that it was in good working order. They carefully labelled crates to ensure that the contents could be readily identified. Personnel of the motor pool checked over their vehicles for mechanical perfection and waterproofed them as necessary.

Eventually the order came to move and the unit departed Hoylake on 13 July 1944, personnel by train, and their vehicles and equipment by road for yet another 'destination unknown'. As their train pulled into the station where they would get off to board army lorries, personnel cast puzzled glances at the familiar surroundings of Bristol Temple Meads station. They boarded lorries for the transfer to their new temporary home and, on arrival, their puzzlement changed to amazement when they found that it was only a few miles from the Tyntesfield hospital they had left only a few months before. This camp was not a marshalling-area camp near to their port of departure, but an intermediate transit camp, the temporary move to free up facilities at Hoylake for other units.

Long Ashton, Somerset, 13 July to 21 July 1944

The annual report for 1944 records the camp as '#9-197, Long Ashton, Somersetshire'. Although no document can be found to more accurately identify the camp location, it is likely to have been in the grounds of the Ashton Court Estate, the ancestral home of the Smythe family. Here, hospital personnel slept, ate and bathed in tented facilities. Ever mindful of the need to move on again at a moment's notice, for the next week they 'kicked their heels', and engaged in the inevitable daily callisthenics.

The feelings of all can be no better expressed than those of the chief nurse:

We lived in pyramidal tents – four or five in a tent – ate from mess kits – how awkward we were washing mess gear! We were issued green combat uniforms and that was our uniforms when we left this staging area. All of our time here was spent writing letters and reading. There is no place in the world which one feels more lonely, unwanted and desperate than at the marshalling area.

On the eighth day after arriving at Long Ashton, the unit moved on again, this time by motor convoy to a marshalling area camp at Broadmayne in the county of Dorset.

Broadmayne, Dorset 21 July to 23 July 1944

As at Long Ashton, the unit's personnel simply 'hung around' awaiting the next order that all knew would be to proceed to the embarkation port. Officers and nurses slept in Nissen huts and enlisted men in pyramidal tents. All personnel exchanged their English money for French, received emergency food rations, and were issued with vomit bags and seasickness tablets.

Eventually, the unit received the order to proceed to Weymouth to board ships that would take them on an overnight crossing of the English Channel to France for 'continental operations'. So, in three marching parties, all but fifty-five men set off from Broadmayne to march the nine miles to the POE [Port of Embarkation]. The other fifty-five men were spared the march by travelling in their vehicles. At Weymouth harbour, one marching party comprising twenty officers, twenty-eight nurses, one physical therapist, one warrant officer, two Red Cross workers and 146 enlisted men boarded LCI-511 [Landing Craft Infantry]; while the other two marching parties comprising thirty-seven officers, fifty-five nurses, two dieticians, one physical therapist, three Red Cross workers and 294 enlisted men boarded LSI-1732 [Landing Ship Infantry]. LSI-1732 was the *SS Leopoldville*, sometimes referred to as *King Leopoldville*, a 12,000-ton Belgian passenger liner converted for use as a troopship. [On Christmas Eve 1944 she was torpedoed by the German submarine U–486 approximately five miles off Cherbourg with the loss of approximately 760 American soldiers.] The vehicle party of four officers and fifty-one enlisted men boarded LST-27 and LST-524 at nearby Portland Harbour.

To minimise the consequences of a ship being sunk and its irreplaceable passengers lost, surgical and medical sections travelled separately.

Lt Col Sheehan, a passenger on the Leopoldville, describes the crossing:

The English Channel, reputedly one of the roughest bodies of water in the world, was, on the occasion of this voyage, almost as placid as a millpond; the weather was clear, and there was no evidence of enemy activity discernable. A most uneventful overnight sailing and the coming of the morning of the 24th brought the vessels in which the marching

SS Leopoldville that took the 74th GH to France. (University of Tennessee)

parties sailed off-shore of the Utah beachhead, here to wait until afternoon for a favorable tide to permit landing.

The Leopoldville anchored offshore and, in the afternoon, its passengers transferred to LCIs and DUKWs to be ferried to the beach. Those who crossed to France in LCIs disembarked directly onto the beach, as described by the chief nurse:

We anchored off Utah beach about 9:00 am. The hundreds of ships lying off the coast was a sight that none of us will ever forget. The channel was buzzing with activity with the continuous unloading of personnel and equipment. About noon, the little LCI pulled up on the beach, dropped the ramp and we marched out onto the beach.

Later in the afternoon of 24 July, the hospital's complement gathered on Utah beach and then quickly moved off to an assembly area a short distance inland from the beachhead. The men marched and the female personnel travelled by motor convoy. At this assembly point, the unit set up a bivouac camp in which it would spend the night.

The following morning, the unit moved on to a staging area 2½ miles south-east of Montebourg, adjacent to where the 8th Field Hospital had earlier been set up. A bivouac area had been cleared of German mines and other ordnance by an engineering unit. All around the cleared area signs stated 'mines cleared to hedges', pointedly implying that there was no guarantee elsewhere. After spending three days at this location, on 28 July the unit moved on by motor convoy to a new location one mile north of Lison where it would set up and eventually operate a general hospital.

Lison, France – 28 July to 23 October 1944

Having arrived at its new location, the first task facing the unit before it could start setting up its camp was to clear the pasture of a herd of sleek, indignant Normandy cows. Similar in many ways to farming areas of the UK, hedgerows separated the fields of the Normandy countryside, so shooing the cows into an adjacent field presented no problem. Their first objective achieved, personnel immediately started work preparing the essential facilities needed for a prolonged stay. They dug latrine and urinal pits, erected tents to house the messes and kitchens, set up ward tents for officers and nurses and shelter tents for enlisted men. Each ward tent provided space for sixteen cots, while the shelter tents accommodated two men sleeping on ground sheets.

Following their arrival in France, many officers, nurses and enlisted men temporarily left the 56th having been assigned on detached service (DS) to field and evacuation hospitals to help out with the immediate treatment of

Lison, France. Main entrance to 56th GH. (56th GH records – NARA)

Lison, France. Two-man shelter tents. (56th GH records – NARA)

Lison, France. Ward tents. (56th GH records – NARA)

Lison, France. Tents – usage unknown. (56th GH records – NARA)

wounded and injured. The numbers of persons on DS peaked on 14 August when twenty-nine of the unit's thirty-six medical officers, seventy-four of its eighty-five nurses and 100 enlisted men were all absent from the unit. Nonetheless, the remaining personnel soon had the camp in a condition fit for human habitation.

Because of the Luftwaffe's nightly heavy aerial activity, all hospital members were urged to dig their own foxhole [shelter trench] into which they could drop to protect themselves from bomb blast.

The chief nurse records:

One girl dug a trench under her cot, the theory being that she could roll right from her bed into the trench.

Ben Dangerfield describes his experience in the first few days:

Almost as soon as we arrived there we began to have nightly visits by a German airplane that we called 'Bed check Charley'. When we heard the plane coming we would run for the closest hedgerow and stay there until it went away. I think it was just reconnaissance but you never know! One night some of us went down the road to a local farmhouse to say hello and have some wine. As we walked along the road back to camp, a German plane was shot down in a field next to where we were walking and one of the big tyres came off and rolled down the road and nearly hit us! We hoped that was the end of 'Bed Check Charley'.

And general living conditions can be gauged from the chief nurse's report:

We ate sitting on the ground and had to fight the bees for every bite. Afternoons we sunbathed, played ping-pong, badminton or volleyball, played cards or did such necessary tasks as laundry or washing the hair – in our helmet of course! Water was not so scarce and was delivered to us in enormous tank trucks.

Using tent poles and tent ropes we rigged up clothes racks around the center tent poles. We covered small areas of the grass floor with boards to put our shoes on to keep them from mildew. We had bedside tables made from steel bomb racks. For lights we used candles or flashlights.

On 2 August 1944, an Engineer General Service Regiment began construction work on what was to be a 1,000-bed general hospital. The site selected for the hospital was to be on the opposite site of a major road from where the hospital's temporary accommodation had been set up. The road, now the D11 – Route d'Isigny – was in constant use by lorries transporting war materials from Cherbourg to the armies south and east. An early and wise decision taken by the planners was to set the hospital site 400 feet from the main road to limit road dirt, dust and noise reaching it. Work progressed steadily but, on 10 August, it ground to a halt when the engineering unit was withdrawn to be deployed elsewhere.

Then, on 11 August, much of the 56th's equipment unexpectedly arrived by rail at Lison station, to be collected by its men and offloaded into a field adjacent to the hospital site. They quickly erected tents in which to temporarily store the equipment, and carefully labelled everything so that it could be readily identified and moved into permanent hospital tents when these were erected. A new engineering regiment arrived on 15 August and work on constructing concrete bases for the permanent tents resumed, following which tents were put up and equipment and beds installed.

The hospital officially opened to receive patients on 1 September with an initial bed capacity of 300, but it was a token occupancy only. Although patients could be put to bed, the hospital could not function properly since no water and electrical systems had been connected; and work on completing operating rooms, X-ray clinic and laboratories had not progressed sufficiently to enable patients to be treated properly. By the opening date, all doctors, nurses and enlisted men who had been on detached service had returned to the parent unit, so over the week following the token opening, all personnel worked hard in getting the hospital fit for purpose. By good fortune, the hospital received no patients until 8 September, at which date also the capacity was raised to 1,000 beds.

During the first week of September, permanent quarters and other facilities were completed, enabling hospital staff to bring to an end the days of living in temporary accommodation. All moved into eight-person tents erected on concrete floors, enlisted men on 6 September and officers and nurses on 9 September, and all tents were rigged with electric lights. In their mess, officers and nurses sat down to eat good food served on proper plates using silverware knives and forks. However, facilities afforded to enlisted men is not recorded in the CO's report. The chief nurse's report records:

> To us our showers seemed luxurious – a ward tent through which passed a pipe with eight shower attachments, duckboards, benches, and not included in the plans – a drier; namely, a 40 mile gale that whipped through the tent constantly!

Following its opening on 8 September, the hospital received and treated wounded and injured in steadily increasing numbers. Most patients arrived by hospital train at Lison station, to be transferred by ambulance to the hospital. The 56th shared the patient load with the 2nd and 25th General Hospitals, also based in the Lison locality. In addition to its influx of American casualties, the hospital started to receive German POW casualties, and gradually their numbers assumed a sizeable proportion of total hospital population. Doctors and nurses found that most American patients they received had generally been well cared for in the field hospitals where they initially received medical aid. By contrast, however, German patients had not been so well cared for, were generally more seriously injured, had travelled much greater distances than Americans, and some required major surgery. Operating also as a station hospital, the 56th treated patients from other American army units stationed nearby.

Lison, France. Wounded being transferred from train to ambulances on route to 56th GH. (56th GH records – NARA)

Some of the not seriously wounded or injured POWs were put to work. Between 12 September and 23 October 1944, 250 of them were employed on mainly minor construction projects: drainage, maintaining paths and roads, etc. None, however, were used in caring for patients or in food preparation or service. When not working, the POWs were confined in a barbed-wire compound, slept in tents, and were constantly guarded by thirty-five to forty of the unit's enlisted men.

On Saturday 7 October 1944, officers and nurses held a party in the officers' club to celebrate the first anniversary of the unit's sailing from Boston to join the war in Europe. An unidentified officer penned a narrative to mark the occasion, entitled 'The March of Time – The Rover Boys in the ETO'.

> *A year ago we crossed the sea*
> *To reach the land of Kings and tea*
> *We've had twelve months of great perfections*
> *(Discounting rain...and all inspections!)*
> *We've learned a lot from the blooming Limey*
> *(You cawn't miss it, you know...blimey!)*
> *We've built more sites and drunk more beers*
> *Than the whole damned lot of engineers*
> *We stayed a while in the Malvern Hills*

And fed NPs a lot of pills
But that type of work was not our kind
So the 56th moved down the line.

At Tyntesfield Park we lived awhile
And covered every walk and aisle
We drank some mild and drank some bitters
And in between we lifted litters
We planted flowers like a public park
And with high headquarters made a mark
But a long, long stay is quite a strain
So we packed once more to board a train!

Then at last we had a break
With private rooms in cold Hoylake
We saw the sights in Liverpool
And sat again in gas-mask school
We took more hikes than the infantry
And drank our gin at the Priory
We saw the cinemas and learned to queue
And tried to study 'parlez vous'.

When General Ike began invading
The 56th needed no persuading
To pack again for travelling Dan'l
And move down close to the Channel
To the Bristol woods again we went
And then at last across were sent.

So here for months we've had a chance
To build up most of northern France
We've wallowed in mud and pastures too
And drowned our sorrows in kick-a-poo
We erected a sign 'bout forty feet wide
The largest thing in the countryside
We set up our club and put in some showers
How long we'll be staying's a matter of hours
For the roads are all built and we've done what we can
Now it's time to load our gypsy van.

But before we go, let's celebrate...
Come on folks, let's congregate...

By the end of September 1944, the fighting front had advanced across France and into Belgium; and much of these two countries had been retaken from the Germans, and Allied forces now stood at the German border on the banks of the River Rhine. Because the fighting front had significantly shifted away from Normandy, American medical authorities decided to move some hospitals closer to the front. Consequently, in the second week of October, Lt Col Sheehan received unofficial notice that the 56th would be on the move.

Shortly thereafter, personnel of the 168th General Hospital arrived and set up their tents in the field where the 56th had camped after first arriving at Lison. Starting on 13 October, most of the new unit's personnel moved into the hospital for training in preparation for the time that they would take over operation of the hospital. By this time, the 56th had received official orders that it was to move from Lison, so at midnight on 23 October 1944, responsibility for operating the Lison hospital passed to the 168th GH.

An advance party of five officers and fifty enlisted men left Lison by motor convoy on 26 October 1944 and headed for their new post at Caserne Fonck, Liège, Belgium.

While at Lison, the 56th admitted 1325 patients of which 454 Americans returned to duty and 501 [Americans and POWs] transferred to other hospitals. Although not stated in reports, the discrepancy in numbers – 370 – was presumably Germans who transferred to POW camps. Four patients died, all POWs. The dispensary and outpatients department saw 1394 patients and administered 2678 treatments.

Liege, Belgium – Caserne Fonck. Main internal couyrtyard. (56th GH records – NARA)

Liège, Belgium – Caserne Fonck. Main entrance to 56th GH. (56th GH records – NARA)

Caserne Fonck, Liège – 2 November 1944 to 31 December 1944

The mission of the unit at this new station was to set up and operate a 1,000-bed general hospital. The buildings of Caserne Fonck stood on an island in the River Meuse in a heavily built-up area approximately 500 metres from Liège city centre. The hospital was to be established in buildings that had once been the home of a horse-drawn Field Artillery Post of the Belgian Army; and until about a month before the 56th's advance party arrived, the German Army had used them as a troop garrison. The central building, some 700 years old, had been built as a monastery. In his 1944 report, Lt Col Sheehan lucidly describes what his party found on arrival:

> *The Advance Party, arriving at this station on 28 October 1944, found a group of dingy red brick buildings, built in a rectangular square, with the outer side of the buildings forming the greater part of the wall which completely encircles the entire compound.*
>
> *The appearance of the garrison gives, at first glance, the impression of a hollow square due to a large courtyard which opens on the main entrance gate, but this impression is proved false upon entering the grounds as two long avenues run between buildings from the courtyard to the opposite encircling wall.*

A parade ground lay at the centre of the complex, surrounded by a number of buildings, and the whole enclosed within a high wall. Widely spread buildings were converted to provide sleeping quarters for all ranks. On the first and second floors of three other buildings, rooms were converted to provide wards, with patient capacities varying from two to twenty-five. Another separate large building was modified to provide accommodation for German POWs. Ground floor stables were converted to house all the other essential departments: operating suite, clinics, laboratory, messes, administration, receiving and evacuation, post exchange (PX), and mail room.

A preliminary survey of all the buildings the 56th would need to convert and adapt were found to be dispiritingly filthy, especially the stables. Undaunted, the advance party first got to work to clear the accumulation of many years' dirt and debris from those buildings designated as staff quarters to make them habitable for the main party when it arrived.

On 1 November, the main party arrived and immediately started clearing the other buildings needed for the hospital to set up its many departments. All personnel, aided by about 200 mostly unskilled civilians, worked tirelessly, though perhaps not enthusiastically. In the stables, removing stall partitions, hay racks, oat basins and harness bars was completed without undue difficulty; cleaning the stable floors, however, proved to be much more challenging. Over many years, horse manure had built up and solidified into a three-foot thick rock-like substance. All attempts to break up this material, even using compressed-air drills, failed to make a significant impression so work was abandoned, and a thick concrete slab cast over it as a seal.

Having cleared the buildings, the unit's next task was to convert and equip them suitable for occupation by the various departments. To achieve this, on 13 November, an Engineer General Service Regiment started work on the project. Construction proceeded at a good pace, but much work was still to be done when, on 20 November 1944, the hospital was told that it was to open immediately for reception of patients. It was officially designated as a 'holding hospital' with a 300-bed capacity, operating on a ten-day evacuation policy.

An extract from the nurses' report describes conditions and their initial thoughts about the new posting:

> *The nurses' quarters had been occupied by German troops, consequently, were filthy, but we were also happy to be in a building again and have a few conveniences of a real home. We marvelled at having such common things as a floor, the windows and a bathroom. The clanging of the streetcars and the shouting of the newsboys were music to our ears.*
>
> *We started immediately to fix the rooms with bits of wallpaper, paint and colorful bedspreads and the work has been continued until now each room has been painted the color requested by the girls living in it.*

We have a lovely dayroom complete with overstuffed furniture, fireplace, rugs and indirect lighting. The mess hall was beautiful and for the first time, we had waitresses to serve us. Directly across from the mess was the clubroom, which with little effort made an ideal officer's club and library.

Our favorite pastime when we first arrived was window shopping. We bought fresh fruit and vegetables in the markets and had our first ice-cream. We went to dances two or three times a week and there were several movie theaters downtown as well as one on the post.

At this opening date, operating a 300-bed hospital and giving patients the care they needed proved to be impossible since the 56th was simply not ready. The bulk of its equipment was still en-route from Normandy. For the first patients, shortage of blankets, essential drugs and other supplies meant that the hospital could provide little more than a bed, food and change of dressings. Doctors performed surgery in extremely inadequate conditions, with only one gasoline autoclave available in which to sterilize surgical instruments. So a party of the unit's most determined men set off in lorries to visit a recently abandoned German hospital at Aachen to relieve it of redundant equipment and other supplies. The party returned with beds, mattresses, operating lights and other useful modern equipment, so enabling the hospital to treat its future patients more efficiently. The unit's remaining equipment and other supplies arrived by rail on 23 November and was unloaded and transferred to the hospital next day.

Lt Col Sheehan reported:

The arrival of this shipment with its urgently needed supply of beds, linen, mattresses, drugs, and surgical dressings and instruments was providential. On 24 November the patient load jumped to over 700 by the reception of patients evacuated from the 15th General Hospital when that installation was hit by an enemy flying bomb.

As Lt Col Sheehan noted, notional bed capacity was raised to 700 on 24 November and further raised to 1,000 on 15 December though the latter capacity was never realised. The increased number of patients inevitably created staffing difficulties. All personnel worked from eight to fourteen hours a day with little time for further training or recreation. To ease the non-medical staffing situation, the hospital took on a number of civilians and, from the last week of November all through December, it employed thirty-four skilled workers – one accountant, two interpreters, thirty-one various building tradesmen; and it employed thirty unskilled workers – three labourers, nine waitresses, six chambermaids and twelve charwomen. Also, during this same period, the hospital employed 200 German POWs to perform similar tasks to those at Lison. The POWs were quartered in what had formerly been a riding arena; and, as at Lison, thirty-five to forty of the unit's enlisted men guarded them.

Before 17 November, V-1 pilotless flying bombs, commonly called 'buzz bombs', had overflown Liège heading for more distant targets but, on that date, Liège became a target with large numbers of V-1s falling night and day. At least fifty landed on the city most days until the end of the month, and an estimated maximum of 140 landed in one day. As the CO reported, on 24 November, the first V-1 fell on the installation of the 15th General Hospital, its near two-ton high-explosive warhead causing extensive damage. Ironically, the first casualties the 56th received at its new location were four duty ambulance drivers from the bombed 15th GH. On arrival, one was found to be dead, one was seriously injured, and the other two were slightly injured. The bomb also destroyed four ambulances of that hospital. Then, for the first two weeks of December, came a respite from the bombardment, only to resume on 16 December and to continue right through the first weeks of February 1945. And in addition to V-1 flying bombs, V-2 supersonic rockets, also carrying a near two-ton high-explosive warhead, started to fall on Liège, though in lesser numbers than V-1s. In total, the Germans launched close to 2,800 V-1s and twenty-seven V-2s against Liège, though the numbers that actually fell on the city and exploded are not known. Statistics compiled after the war concluded that the pilotless bombs destroyed or damaged 67,000 of Liège's buildings, the

V-1 in flight.

Liege, Belgium – Caserne Fonck. Views of houses demolished by V-1 on 17 December 1944.
(Jim Scott – son of Robert Scott)

city sustaining greater damage than either London or Antwerp.

Lt Col Sheehan recorded:

> *While everyone went about his job as efficiently as he could, it cannot be denied that nearly everyone developed a 'big ear' from listening for the sputtering motor sound of the buzz bombs.*

And the hospital's patients loathed the bombing. Soldiers in the field were trained to take cover in slit trenches when being shelled or bombed but, lying in hospital beds, many of them unable to move, all they could do was to suffer the severe mental anguish and pray, since moving them was clearly impracticable.

And Ben Dangerfield recalls:

> *You would hear the droning of one coming over, and if that noise stopped you ran for cover. The whistling sound told you how close it was. I was in the shower one morning when a buzz bomb landed in the house across the alley, destroying the house and its occupants plus other houses.*

The V-1 to which Ben referred fell at 11:00 am on 17 December and, as well as destroying houses, it also damaged hospital buildings. The explosion caused structural damage to two ward blocks so their patients had to be moved into other wards. Many other buildings sustained minor damage with plaster falling from walls and ceilings, and glass shattering in about seventy-five per cent of all windows in hospital buildings. Fortunately, patients and hospital personnel suffered only minor abrasions and cuts from falling plaster and flying glass.

Resulting from the closure of the two damaged wards, the hospital was forced to lower its bed capacity to 850, and this limit continued until the end of December 1944. Moreover, the need to repair buildings that had suffered damage from the explosion set back the hospital's completion date by an estimated forty days.

The chief nurse, in her end-of-war report, graphically depicts the awful working conditions at the time:

> *We wore fatigues until we got the hospital operating and then we changed to seersucker uniforms. However, they proved impractical during the buzz-bomb siege because of the cold due to windows being knocked out, the dirt from falling plaster and the necessity of 'hitting' the floor when a bombs motor cut out directly overhead, so we went back to fatigues.*
>
> *Here we were in a beautiful location with comforts and advantages rarely enjoyed overseas – and then came the flying bombs! Only those people who have endured an aerial attack of V-1s and V-2s can know the horror of such weapons. During this period nothing could entice us to leave camp. Not that our camp was safe, but there was a feeling of security in being with your friends.*
>
> *We were tired, nervous and afraid and there was an obvious tenseness indicated by everyone's manner. For the first time we really knew what it was to live only for that day; tomorrow was always doubtful.*

For the first half of December, for the most part the hospital continued to operate as a 'holding hospital', but then, on 16 December, its role fundamentally changed when the Germans opened their last-ditch offensive in the Ardennes, the so-called Battle of the Bulge. Prior to that date, staff had coped well with the numbers of admittances and evacuations with 521 beds occupied. But then admittances rose significantly, with 80 to 170 battle casualties arriving each day and requiring treatment by the surgical service. Right through the Ardennes conflict, the hospital regularly received casualties suffering from trench foot, from shrapnel wounds, and many simply from battle exhaustion. German POWs especially suffered from trench foot with gangrenous toes and sometimes whole feet, in some cases so severe that amputation was the only option. Nonetheless, the unit dealt with its patients efficiently and took pride in being able to return thirty per cent of American soldiers they treated back to full duty within the ten-day evacuation period.

Normally, general hospitals were sensibly sited well back from the front

Liege, Belgium – Caserne Fonck. Captain Robert Scott, second left, celebrating Christmas day 1944 with a Belgian family. (Jim Scott – son of Robert Scott)

line, receiving their patients mainly from evacuation hospitals. But during the Battle of the Bulge, the Germans advanced to within fourteen miles of Liège. Consequently, the 56th started to receive wounded by ambulance direct from aid stations at the front, and this continued right through January 1945. In ideal circumstances, the 56th and other hospitals in the Liège area would have been evacuated farther back from the fighting, but roads and rail lines were in no fit state on which to move patients so they were trapped. But then, on 27 January 1945, as the Allies gained ground and the front line moved farther away from Liège, numbers of casualties arriving direct from field hospitals reduced. Increasingly, more were transported by airlift and hospital train from evacuation hospitals.

The hospital continued to operate with an 850-bed capacity until 17 January when it was again increased to 1,000. With the outcome of the war inevitable, the need to return patients to duty lessened so the evacuation policy increased to twenty days on 1 February, and to sixty days on 1 March.

By 19 January 1945, all hospital departments were functioning efficiently in their new quarters, helping to lighten the burden on all personnel, but the overall shortage of surgeons and nurses meant that they routinely worked a twelve-hour day with few breaks, and sometimes as long as twenty hours a day. Consequently, nurses relied more and more on enlisted medical technicians to assist them in giving plasma, penicillin and sulpha drugs, and changing dressings. And the hospital's five Red Cross ladies worked tirelessly in providing the same service to all patients that they had done at Tyntesfield.

Yet, despite the high workload in the early months of 1945, numbers of hospital personnel generally reduced as some were transferred to other hospital units and some returned home to the States. Over the first five months of 1945, Medical Corp officers reduced in number from thirty-five to twenty-nine; nurses reduced from eighty-two to seventy-nine; and enlisted men reduced from 458 to 442. But the Dental Corp and the Administrative Corp were more fortunate, the dentists maintaining their numbers at six throughout and the administrators increasing their numbers from six to ten.

To ease the problems caused by staff shortage, during those first five months of 1945 the hospital took on an additional sixty-nine civilians, twenty-nine of them skilled workers employed as accountants, painters, electricians, plumbers, carpenters, seamstresses and tailors. The other forty, many of them unskilled women, were employed as waitresses, charwomen and kitchen helpers. In the same period, the hospital made use of 264 POWs mostly employed in fairly menial jobs, but thirty-four were employed as medical technicians. The latter group, previously trained medical personnel in the German Army, proved very useful because of the large number of wounded German POWs in the hospital who spoke no English.

With the approach of spring 1945, the V-1 and V-2 onslaught ceased as the launching sites were overrun by the Allies advance, so life for hospital personnel became much less stressful. Construction work, repairs and general improvements in the hospital having been completed, nurses were able to cast off their fatigues and return to wearing more feminine seersucker uniforms. Also, with a significant drop in the numbers of patients needing full-time nursing, groups of nurses were allowed time off, some visiting Brussels, Paris, England and the French Riviera. And as the weather improved, excursions

Liege, Belgium – Caserne Fonck. German POWs transferring patients to an ambulance.
(56th GH records– NARA)

174

Liege, Belgium – Caserne Fonck. Dodge ambulances. (56th GH records – NARA)

and picnics for staff and ambulatory patients were held on boats sailing on the River Meuse, with the hospital orchestra often providing the music.

In April 1945, Belgian authorities provided further assistance to ease the hospital's shortage of enlisted men by making available a battalion of Territorial soldiers to guard German POWs: one officer, one warrant officer and twenty-seven enlisted men.

Lt Col Sheehan observed:

> *On the whole, this arrangement proved entirely unsatisfactory from the hospital's point of view. The Belgian Territorials – a military Home Guard – attached to the hospital was unaggressive, unsoldierly, lazy and prone to treat the POWs they were guarding too leniently.*
>
> *But while the arrangement was unsatisfactory, it did release the unit's own men to do their proper jobs.*

On 12 February 1945, Lt Col Sheehan was promoted to the rank of full colonel and, on 18 April 1945, his role as CO of the 56th ended when he was assigned to the 810th Medical Services Hospital Center in Paris as Chief of Training in the Operations Division. Then, on 28 March 1946, he was relieved of that assignment and became Chief Officer, Operations Division in the Office of the Chief Surgeon, in Germany. Shortly thereafter, sometime in April 1946, Col Sheehan returned to the US to work in the office of the Surgeon General in Washington, DC.

As Allied forces advanced into Germany, they discovered POW camps. Following their release, POWs [officially called RAMPS – Recovered Allied Military Personnel] were first given a health check and treatment if required. So, probably in March but the actual date is not recorded in the CO's report, the 56th was designated to care for released Allied prisoners-of-war. Few of those who arrived at the 56th needed surgical or extensive medical treatment, though some were suffering from respiratory problems and tuberculosis. However, most showed clear signs of malnourishment. Their diet and intake of food and drink in hospital was carefully specified and controlled by the hospital dietician, and most gradually gained weight and good health. Through the remaining months of the war and until the unit's closure in July 1945, RAMPS outnumbered patients transferred from other hospitals.

Maj. Gen Paul Hawley presenting Legion of Merit medal to Col. Daniel Sheehan, 21 June 1945. (Molly Placko)

Over the first five months of 1945, the numbers of patients admitted monthly were 3,285, 2,450, 4,556, 1,718, 1,099 – a total of 13,108. In the same period, the number of patients returned to duty with their units was 2,743, and those transferred to other hospital totalled 1,155. 5,927 patients were evacuated elsewhere by hospital train, 983 by air, and thirty-six patients died. In the same five–month period, 266 of those admitted were suffering with psychiatric problems; sixty-seven of them returned to full duty with their units, nine to limited assignments, and 190 were transferred to specialist hospitals for continuing treatment. In the same five-month period of operation, at 11,849 sittings, the dental department treated 418 inpatients, 2,755 outpatients, extracted 1,405 teeth, and filled a further 3,426 teeth. And in the same period, the dispensary saw 7,957 outpatients and administered 12,860 treatments.

Col Sheehan's successor as CO of the 56th GH is not recorded, nor can the date of the hospital's return to the United States be found in official records. The only information that can be found relating to the unit's final days following WWII is in 'Maryland in World War II – Volume I Military Participation' published in 1950, which states:

> The members of the 56th saw the European campaign to its finish, and then some of them were ordered back to the United States, where, in November 1945, at the Hampton Roads Port of Embarkation [Virginia], the hospital was deactivated.

During its time of operations under enemy fire on mainland Europe, the unit lost one member killed, one seriously wounded and forty-three slightly wounded.

Finally, perhaps no better concluding comments on the 56th's time in the UK, France and Belgium can be offered, no doubt representing the feelings of most hospital personnel, than those of the chief nurse in her end-of-war report:

> *Each nurse has lived through an era of happiness, of loneliness, of difficulties, of gay fun, of hard work; all intermingled with valuable experience and education. Like typical soldiers, we have 'griped' but whenever there was a job to be done, we responded enthusiastically and rendered the best professional care possible. Adjustment to overseas life has not been easy, but most of the girls have done an excellent job. In short, we feel that we gave our soldiers a good nursing care and we are proud of the job we have done.*

Chapter Fourteen

The 74th GH After Tyntesfield

When the 74th left Tyntesfield, all that was positively known about its future was that it was heading for France where its mission was to '...provide treatment for patients evacuated from local field hospitals and provide station-hospital facilities for patients from nearby areas'. Arriving at Bristol Temple Meads station, personnel settled themselves on the train that would take them to Southampton docks and the ship that awaited them. Three hours after arriving at Southampton, they boarded the converted liberty ship *Marine Wolf* and weighed anchor at 1:30 in the afternoon and, following an uneventful crossing, the ship tied up at Le Havre docks the same evening. All of the hospital staff remained on board until the following afternoon, eventually disembarking at 3:00 pm on Wednesday 27 June 1945. They were given a hot meal in an army mess hall near the railway station, and then climbed into '40 and 8s' railway boxcars to travel to a transit camp at Etretat, France, where they arrived at 9:00 in the evening. [The term '40 and 8s'

Marine Wolf that took 74th GH across to Le Havre, France. (University of Tennessee)

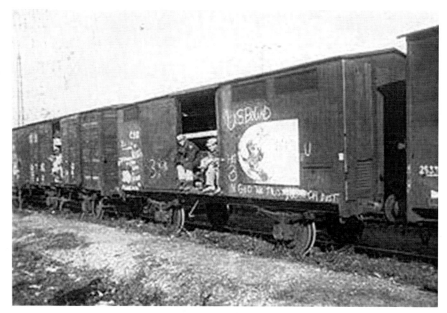

40 & 8 French Railway Boxcar.

comes from the French designation '40 *hommes et 8 cheveaux*' which means the boxcars had a capacity of forty men or eight horses].

After the liberation of Le Havre on 12 September 1944, the port became a major entry point in France for American troops, and the Americans needed staging (transit) camps in the vicinity of the port. Consequently, they established a dozen or so camps in the area, all of which were code-named after American cigarette brands. The camp at Etretat was named 'Pall Mall'. A coastal town in the Haute-Normandie region, Etretat lay some twenty miles north-east of Le Havre.

In late 1944, when the camps were set up, they provided mostly tented accommodation with rudimentary bathing facilities, and were sarcastically dubbed 'pneumonia holes' by soldiers who lodged in them. Although no detailed information can be found about how 'Pall Mall' might have improved by June 1945, its austere living conditions would likely not have changed greatly. Officer personnel of the 74th slept in cots set up in large tents while other ranks slept on ground sheets in squad tents.

In a letter to her mother dated 29 June 1945, nurse Alice Boehret describes the process of bathing at 'Pall Mall':

You should have seen us last night taking a bath in our helmets. It was really rare. The basin (helmet) was hung by the chin strap to the pole on the army cot and you sat on the bed and bathed. More fun! Tonight though, I guess I'll walk the half mile on those awful stones and take a shower. A soldier is posted in front of the shower room to keep the officers and men from just walking in.

The unit stayed at Etretat for only forty-two hours for, on Friday 29 June 1945 at 3:00 pm, personnel again climbed up into boxcars and departed for the town of St Quentin, arriving at 5:00 the next morning. St Quentin was to be the hospital's first 'permanent' station in France.

St Quentin, France – 30 June 1945 to 10 August 1945

At St Quentin railway station, the unit's personnel once again clambered up into army lorries which, an hour later, dropped them at a large school: the Lycee Henri Martin. The school comprised three-storey buildings, built in the shape of a square letter 'A'. When the 74th arrived, work was underway to improve plumbing and other facilities, and all the rooms were being repainted. Two weeks later, work having been completed, the buildings looked cheerful and spotless, and personnel immediately got to work on setting up the various departments.

In the main school building, the unit set up nine wards for the surgical and medical services, with a capacity of 560 beds. In addition, to raise the capacity to close to the 1,000 beds required, fourteen ward tents were set up in an athletics field adjoining the main building, each tent holding thirty beds. Two of the tents were used for German POW casualties, and four were held in readiness for a mass admittance, but never actually required. As

St. Quentin, France. 74th GH accommodation in the school Lycee Henri Martin. (University of Tennessee)

at Tyntesfield, convalescing and ambulatory patients mostly occupied ward tents. Separate wards were allocated for officers and nurses: six large rooms with a total of fifty-six beds for officers, and one room for female patients, though no more than two females ever occupied beds at any one time.

The grounds of the school offered pleasant surroundings to lighten the gloom. They contained a number of enclosed courtyards and gardens, with a mature chestnut tree standing in the centre of each grassed area. Another courtyard contained a beautiful rose garden divided into quarters by cross walks. The rose garden provided an excellent open-air location for outdoor Red Cross activities; patients worked at handicrafts, played cards, read and generally relaxed in the congenial atmosphere.

Male officers and nurses were billeted in the dormitory building of the nearby Institute St Jean, but no personnel were quartered in the Lycee Henri Martin school buildings. As was the usual practice, enlisted men slept in squad tents set up in the grounds of a sports stadium near to the main hospital building.

Before the 74th arrived at St Quentin, the 228th GH ran the hospital. This unit immediately handed over responsibility to the 74th on its arrival and the next day, Sunday 1 July 1945, the 228th left St Quentin for deployment elsewhere. Another American General Hospital, the 197th, operating elsewhere in St Quentin at that time, also closed immediately, transferring its patients to the 74th.

The 74th officially opened at one minute past midnight on 1 July 1945, operating a 1,000-bed general hospital and receiving its first patients the following day. From a letter to sister Dorothy written by Alice Boehret on 5 July, it is clear that some of the wards were set up in very large rooms. The letter also shows that the nurses maintained a good sense of humour:

> At dinner tonight we almost laughed ourselves sick. We were trying to devise a system where the nurses wouldn't wear themselves out running up and down the wards. One ward has eighty-five beds in it in four rows, so you can see that there is a problem. First we thought roller skates would do. After all they use them in the Senate. Then bicycles was [sic] thought up. Someone suggested dogs with a bottle of cognac around their necks and messages attached to be sent down the rows.

The 74th's first patients to occupy beds arrived on 2, 3 and 4 July when 449 patients transferred from the now-closed 197th GH; 236 of these were surgical cases, and the other 213 medical. The 213 medical cases included twelve neuro-psychiatric cases, thirty-five officer medical patients, and thirty-five German POWs with mixed medical needs. Following this initial influx, the daily intake of patients averaged about sixteen for both of the services. During the period of operation at St Quentin, forty to forty-five per cent of all patients were medical cases, including neuro-psychiatric, the remainder being surgical cases. The highest census of inpatients for the entire hospital was 484 on 30 July.

Although patients were mainly classified as surgical or medical cases, a number of other separately classified services operated in the hospital. These included an outpatients' consultation section, a GU (geinto-urinary) service, EENT (eyes, ears, nose and throat) and the dental service. The number of outpatient consultations is not recorded, but a known forty-seven neuro-psychiatric patients were seen. The GU service received thirty patients from the 197th GH when that unit closed, and it continued to see and treat VD cases from army units stationed in the area. The dental service comprised five officers and ten technicians, and also employed the services of four German POWs: one dentist and three dental technicians. From 1 July to 5 August, dental workers examined 684 patients, inserted 447 fillings, extracted 139 teeth, made and fitted forty-two full sets of dentures and 109 partial dentures, and repaired a further twenty sets of dentures.

An unusual situation is recorded in the CO's report concerning a soldier who sustained a serious gunshot wound to his abdomen. The wounding occurred forty miles away from the 74th's hospital, and the soldier was judged too seriously ill to be moved to the hospital. Although full details of where and how he was wounded are not included, the report records that a complete medical service and its equipment was sent to him from the 74th. However, despite valiant efforts by doctors and nurses, sadly he died one week after being wounded.

Patients who passed through the various hospital services returned either to their original units, transferred to what were called reinforcement depots, or were transferred back to the United States (Z of I – Zone of Interior). Reinforcement depots were camps where soldiers whose original units had moved on elsewhere awaited posting to other units as required. During the twenty-nine days the hospital operated, of the ten officers and eighty-five non-officer ranks who returned to the States, the majority were neuro-psychiatric cases who returned direct to the Z of I. In addition, in the period from 17 to 28 July, another 142 patients initially transferred to the 55th and 94th GHs for further processing before onward transfer to the States.

Recreation time was important for staff and patients alike, and most of the facilities provided at Tyntesfield within the hospital and in nearby Bristol were available at St Quentin. Staff and able patients took part in all the usual outdoor sporting activities, and leagues were organised among various units in the area for baseball, volleyball and horseshoe pitching [a pastime where the aim was to throw a horseshoe from a distance to land over a steel pin driven into the ground]. The hospital band regularly received requests to perform at venues throughout the area for dances playing genuine 'solid American swing' music;

and they played at the weekly dances organised for hospital staff. Also, with the lighter workload, many of the staff were given the opportunity for sightseeing and visited many towns in France, Belgium and the surrounding countryside.

But probably the most popular form of entertainment was watching the 'motion picture'. When the Americans liberated St Quentin in September 1944, they set up in the town a cinema with up-to-date equipment showing 35mm feature films. This picture house, called *The Splendid,* served all Allied troops in the area, and casual ones passing through. The cinema seated 1,500 with a film shown every night, and with two changes of film each week. Total weekly admissions numbered approximately 2,500. When the 74th arrived in town, it took over running the cinema. To provide a better service, three new films were shown each week with two complete shows every night and an additional matinee on Sundays, resulting in a jump in total weekly attendances to 4,500. For patients in hospital who could not get to the cinema in town, the American Special Services unit set up a 300-seat cinema in the school showing 16mm films. Films were shown three times every day, with three programme changes each week.

In planning for post-war employment for many thousands of service personnel who would return to civilian life, the hospital set up an Information and Education (I & E) group. This group came into being at Tyntesfield on 18 May 1945 and continued to operate when the unit transferred to France. It ran courses in many diverse subjects including spoken French, advanced French, automobile mechanics, livestock production, crop management and soil conservation. And, in July 1945, two enlisted men attended a course in teacher training at the *Cite Universitaire* in Paris.

Although Allied forces at the time were often referred to as the 'Army of Occupation', the term did not technically apply to France. Nonetheless, the Allies did provide management expertise in helping the country to get back 'on its feet' after the war. Staff from the 74th GH ran a number of the town's facilities until local people could confidently take over the work from the Americans. These included five hotels, two petrol filling stations, the city water supply and two vegetable farms. The surgical service also provided officers to investigate civilian traffic accidents involving US personnel.

Then, on 10 August 1945, its work done at St Quentin, the 74th moved on again by motor convoy to its next posting at Mourmelon, France.

Mourmelon, France – 11 August 1945 to 24 August 1945

In Col Teperson's report covering 1945, he refers to this post as being at *Mourmelon*, France. Two towns approximately seventeen miles south-east of Rheims include *Mourmelon* in their names: *Mourmelon-le-Grand* and *Mourmelon-le-Petit*, so the 74th's new assignment was doubtless in or near to one of these towns. The military post at Mourmelon was part of a staging area adjoining Rheims and covered a huge area. The camp contained a number of hospital units as well as other American military units, and experienced a constant coming and going of personnel. The 74th was not given its own hospital to operate at this station, but provided officers, nurses and enlisted men on temporary duties (TD) to assist the resident 55th GH.

Col Teperson records that housing his staff presented an initial problem due to general overcrowding. However, to a large extent, the problem solved itself when a sizeable number of the 74th's personnel, not needed at this station, were placed on detached service to other hospitals. As at other posts, enlisted men slept in tents in the hospital grounds.

One of the nurses on detached service was Alice Boehret with the 79th GH at Sissonne, who wrote to her mother on 11 August 1945:

> *Here we are on D. S. because our hospital is closed. It is a rather nice set-up, in a French Cavalry school.*
>
> *Things are really stewing at the 74th now. We don't know if we will rejoin or not. There are only 24 nurses left and we are farmed out. I'm on duty on the orthopedic ward. I do believe more men are breaking their legs playing baseball than were shot in the same given time.*

And in another letter written on 14 August 45 to sister Dorothy:

> *We all want to return to the 74th. This Detached Service ain't all it's cracked up to be. Besides at the 74th we wouldn't have to work at all. And here we do. I never knew so many men could break their legs playing baseball. That game is a menace to society.*

Assisting the 55th GH in operating the hospital proved to be short-lived for, on 21 August 1945, Col Teperson received orders to prepare the unit for another move, this time to Commercy to take over responsibility for a hospital then being run by the 50th GH. On 24 August, after hurriedly packing its equipment and paperwork, the 74th's personnel once again clambered up into a convoy of lorries that would take them to their new post.

Commercy, France – 24 August 1945 to 19 November 1945

The new base at Commercy, in a complex of buildings called *Caserne Oudinot*, had once housed soldiers of the French Cavalry. The first hospital set up by the Americans at this station was the 50th GH. On arrival late in November 1944, its hospital personnel immediately saw that the buildings were totally unfit for purpose. Supply and distribution of water and electricity, plumbing and heating were all ancient and totally inadequate for hospital needs and would have to be replaced. Fortunately for the 74th, when it arrived all of the changes and improvements had been completed, and wards and the numerous other departments were well established. Wards and other rooms were heated using tent stoves converted for burning oil since no central heating had been installed, but each building had its own boiler to provide hot water at all times. The surrounding grounds had been landscaped and included many flowerbeds, lawns and trees. With beds for 2,370 patients, the hospital would be the largest the 74th had ever operated.

Quarters and messes for all ranks were described by Col Teperson as '...adequate and comfortable and it was a pleasure for the enlisted men to put away their mess gear and use trays and silverware which were furnished'. Bathing and laundry facilities were also better than at any other post where the 74th had operated, with hot showers available at all times. An American quartermaster laundry unit located in Commercy took care of all clothes' washing and cleaning.

Formal transfer of the hospital from the 50th to the 74th officially took place at one minute past midnight on 27 August 1945 when the patient census stood at 660. Of the 660, few were battle casualties, the majority suffering from various medical conditions, mainly acute respiratory infections with tonsillitis predominating. About eighty patients in the hospital when the 74th took over included American RAMPS, soldiers of the Polish, Italian, British and Yugoslav armies, and French and Luxembourg civilians. Of the RAMPS, many had contracted tuberculosis in their prison camps.

When the 74th assumed responsibility for the hospital, its nursing strength stood at an insufficient eighteen. However, to provide the required level of care, twenty-five nurses from 50th GH remained on temporary duty. As time passed and patient numbers dwindled, although a few nurses left, the ratio of nurses to patients climbed because the scattered location of buildings and their wards necessitated the high ratio.

Only about six new patients arrived each day, most from two field hospitals, the 46th in Luxembourg and the 78th at Verdun, and from other US Army installations in the area. New patients were admitted generally for observation, a few for treatment, and others to be medically assessed for suitability to return to the United States. The outpatients' department continued to deal with VD cases, seeing an average twenty-five patients every day. During the last two weeks of operation, dispositions exceeded admissions when the daily census never exceeded fifty patients.

The unit employed 483 German POWs throughout the hospital, mostly on menial duties. In the wards and barracks, they cleaned floors and windows; in the kitchens, they prepared mounds of vegetables; in mess halls, they served coffee at the tables; and, in the grounds, they kept everything neat and clean. The unit also employed 130 Poles and 109 French civilians as guards for the POWs, as interpreters, and in general labouring tasks.

As at every other base in the European Theatre of Operations, the dental service was never short of patients. Between 27 August and 19 November, its officers and technicians examined 992 patients who required no treatment, filled 458 teeth, extracted 124 teeth, made and fitted twenty-three full denture sets and ninety-eight partial, repaired sixty-five dentures, and performed 325 other minor treatments.

In the months leading up to the hospital's closure, as at St Quentin and when time allowed, all ranks were given the opportunity to study many diverse subjects to prepare for their post-war future. This opportunity to study new subjects was particularly valuable to enlisted men, many having entered the army straight from school and the only 'trade' they knew was war-related.

When the 74th took over operating the hospital from the 50th, it also took over responsibility for running five farms together with the farm labour comprising mostly Polish displaced persons and German POWs. Vegetables grown on the farms supplemented the hospital's mess requirements. As crops were gathered in, the farms were handed back to their owners and casual labour discharged.

From about early September 1945, with diminishing patient admissions, many of the unit's officers, nurses and enlisted men became surplus to needs; some transferred to other hospitals and others returned to the United States. Notable among those who had sailed on the *Queen Mary* to travel to the ETO and were now homeward bound were the commanding officer, Col Hyman Teperson; the chief nurse, Major Margaret Hornickel; and nurse Lt Alice Boehret, all of whom departed in mid-September. After this latest departure of personnel, only six of the ninety-five nurses who had sailed down the Hudson River on the *Queen Mary* on 1 March 1944 remained with the unit. Following the departure of Col Teperson, Lt Col Elisha D Embree, who had commanded three other hospitals during the war, assumed command of the 74th on 18 September 1945. He had previously been executive officer of the 74th and was already well known to the personnel who were happy to have him as CO.

During the 74th's time at Commercy, four soldiers died: a German POW, a Polish Army soldier and two Italian POWs, all from pneumonia, hepatitis or respiratory problems.

Throughout September, October and the first two weeks of November, the patient census continued to drop, and American authorities decided to close the hospital. Therefore, on 19 December 1945, the 74th's last patients left the hospital, to be discharged from care or evacuated to the 68th GH (location unknown). The hospital formally closed at midnight that same day. Some members of the units remained at Commercy in a 'guarding' role for a while after closing and, on 1 December, seventeen officers and ninety enlisted men comprised its official strength. But, of that total, only seven officers and fifty-five enlisted men were available for duty, the others being on temporary duties or detached service with other outfits.

Then, on 2 and 8 December, the depleted personnel of the unit moved on again by motor transport back to Mourmelon-le-Grand; one officer and twelve enlisted men remaining behind at *Caserne Oudinot* to hand over the site to the French authorities. Back at Mourmelon-le-Grand, hospital personnel moved into an existing hospital but, with no patients to look after, its function was mainly one of guarding and maintaining the site. Over the following months, various officers and enlisted men transferred elsewhere and, on 1 December, only six officers remained on the 74th's roster, and only three were available for duty. Between 1 December and 26 December, new commanding officers were appointed on three occasions, some holding the post for only a few days, the last recorded CO being Capt Joseph N Cutler who took command on 26 December 1945.

In the period from the closing date at *Caserne Oudinot* to the end of December, the unit lost nineteen officers and forty-one nurses. Of these, six officers returned Stateside, and the remainder transferred to other hospital units. All forty-one nurses transferred to other hospitals in the ETO. During December, the organisation received a large addition to its enlisted personnel. On 22 December, seventy-one enlisted men were assigned from the 158th GH and, on 30 December, 111 further enlisted men joined from the 189th GH, so that, at the end of the year, the unit's strength stood at six officers and 265 enlisted men. The purpose of the boost in numbers is not recorded in the CO's reports.

A few days before Christmas, two of the 74th's original Red Cross workers returned to the unit to make preparations for its personnel to celebrate Christmas in the traditional way.

Details of the time spent at Mourmelon-le-Grand during December 1945, have been extracted from a report prepared and signed by Capt Joseph N Cutler. Puzzlingly, the report is dated 8 December 1946, almost a year after the events reported. No later report can be found in the US National Archives and Records Administration, nor in the archives of the Surgeon General's or Adjunct General's offices. So, sadly, the ongoing role and locations of the 74th General Hospital after 1945, the return of its personnel to the United States, and the date of its disbandment cannot be established. However, we do know what happened to nurse Lt Alice Boehret.

After leaving the 74th at Commercy, Alice transferred to another unit, the 46th General Hospital based at Besançon, France, a town near the French-Swiss border. In a letter home dated 24 September 1945, Alice implied that Besançon was more of a staging camp than a place of work. At this hospital, nurses from hospital units in the ETO destined to return home gathered for final processing, their records brought up to date, and general health checks carried out.

Alice's next letter, written on 2 October 1945 to her mother, confirms the impression that the nurses at Besançon who were homeward bound did no work but much sightseeing, including a 'little jaunt to the Swiss border'. And Alice also spent a weekend in Paris, taking in all the sights of the city including a trip to Versailles. And in the letter she said:

> *If you get any packages addressed to me from me don't be too surprised because it is champagne in a plaster cast. When I come home we will really celebrate, so don't decide to break the cast. Besides, there is a special way to take those casts off so you don't break the bottle or the seal.*

Eventually, Alice left Besançon by bus to start the eight-hour journey that would take her to Camp Carlisle, near Rheims, France. Camp Carlisle was the nurses' final assembly area prior to returning home, and at the end of October 1945 held about 1,500 nurses, technically still attached to the 46th General Hospital. In her final letter home to her mother, written on 25 October from Camp Carlisle, Alice wrote:

> *This is quite a place. Nothing but women, women everywhere. It is just like old home week because you are always meeting someone from before. And such a gab-fest.*
>
> *We are hoping to make the next crossing of the "Queen Mary". I think that is the only one they carry female personnel on these days. Women are such a bother.*

But Alice did not travel home on the *Queen Mary*. Instead, she and many other nurses, all apparently temporarily attached to the 46th GH, together with soldiers from other American military units, returned to the United States aboard the former Italian cruise liner *SS Vulcania*. The ship sailed from Le Havre on 3 November 1945 and docked in New York harbour on 10 November.

Chapter Fifteen

After the War – The Tyntesfield Village

Early in 1945, the Bristol Health Committee started to look to the future of health care in the city and how its hospital facilities could best be expanded. Minute no 348, dated 24 April 1945, (from the Minute Book of Bristol Health Committee) records that:

> *The Medical Officer for Health had lodged a claim with the Ministry of Health for using the hutted accommodation after the US vacated the site [Tyntesfield] for dealing with acute and maternity cases, tuberculosis and orthopaedic cases. The committee resolved to find out for what period they could have use of the accommodation.*

At the same time, the Health Committee also considered Frenchay hospital as a site that could be developed to provide the additional facilities so desperately needed. Frenchay, like Tyntesfield, was home to American General Hospitals from 1942 until three months after the war's end. The Health Committee's minute 503 – 26 May 1945 – resolved to urge the War Office to release both Tyntesfield and Frenchay hospitals for civilian use as soon as possible after the war ended.

The Health committee set up a sub-committee to look more closely at the merits and demerits of the two hospitals. Although Frenchay hospital dated back to the 1920s when it was opened as a sanatorium and orthopaedic hospital for tuberculosis children, major expansion commenced in 1942 with the construction of new wards and other medical facilities for use by the American Army. Although no specific reasons were stated, it appears from the sub-committee's minute 223, dated 4 September 1945, that interest in Tyntesfield was waning as the committee was not prepared to commit itself to acquiring Tyntesfield.

A minute from Long Ashton Rural District Council meeting on 7 November 1945 records that Bristol Corporation wrote to the council requesting the council's observation on retention of the camp: one, is there need for a permanent hospital in the area, and two, are the buildings suitable to serve that purpose? LARDC replied negatively to both questions, though its reasons for the negative response are not recorded. However, the council did suggest that the camp could be retained to provide temporary housing accommodation.

In late 1945, the Bristol Health Committee took over the control of Frenchay hospital as agents for the Ministry of Health, the last of the Americans having departed on 16 August 1945. And so its interest in using the buildings of the old 74th GH ended.

The birth of Tyntesfield Park

With the departure of the 74th GH from Tyntesfield on 26 June 1945, responsibility for care of the site and buildings passed to the British War Office. In the period from the Americans' departure to the end of 1945, the use of the site is uncertain. A minute from Long Ashton Rural District Council's meeting on 20 November 1945 refers to the camp being used as a transit camp by the military authorities, but who was in transit is not given. And an article in the *Western Daily Press & Bristol Mirror* newspaper for 9 March 1946 states that:

> *After the Americans left the area, Tyntesfield was occupied by a small holding force of 50 British troops, but now the sole occupier of the 100 buildings in the camp is a military caretaker.*

The destruction of many thousands of houses throughout the UK by German bombs resulted in large numbers of people simply having nowhere to live. This predicament gave rise early in 1946 to what became know as the *squatting* phenomenon. After the war's end, hundreds of military and prisoner-of-war (POW) camps throughout the UK, including many around the Bristol area, were evacuated, and homeless families, the so-called *squatters*, moved in. Some local people insist that the Tyntesfield hospital site also became home to squatters, but there is no indication in LARDC minutes that this was so. The fifty troops referred to in the newspaper article may have been based there temporarily before moving on elsewhere (in transit), or they may simply have been stationed at the camp to guard it and prevent squatters moving in. Also, some locals contend that Polish families were temporarily housed there immediately following the war's end before being resettled at Ilford Park, near Newton Abbot, Devon. However, the Devon camp did not open as a Polish exiles' resettlement camp until 1948, so this contention does not tally with the facts.

What is fact, however, is that sometime towards the end of 1945 or the beginning of 1946, LARDC initiated a proposal to convert the camp buildings into temporary homes to help solve the chronic local housing shortage. At a meeting of LARDC on 6 March 1946, the Clerk reported that:

> *Representatives of LARDC had visited the camp to establish whether it was suitable for conversion into temporary civilian accommodation.*

The minutes record a resolution:

...that immediate steps be taken to requisition the camp.

The committee also suggested that part of the camp might be used as a temporary secondary school, and as a teachers' training school until proper facilities could be built.

On 12 April 1946, the War Office transferred the site and its buildings to the British Ministry of Works (MOW), who at the time was acting caretaker, until its future use could be decided. Although not strictly responsible for the site, LARDC maintained a close interest in its future and recommended that Mr Rich, a civilian who had been the foreman of the maintenance staff for the MOW during the American residence, be retained because of his knowledge of the water and sewerage systems. Mr Rich was subsequently appointed on a salary of £6-10s per week, plus allowances towards his travelling expenses. Seven men who had worked in Mr Rich's hospital maintenance team were also taken on by the MOW to assist him. In addition, the MOW agreed to appoint a full-time caretaker to look after the premises at night-time and weekends.

Almost immediately following the end of World War II, close to five million men and women who had served in the British armed forces were declared redundant. The demobilization of this vast force and their resettlement back into civilian life was one of the first and greatest challenges facing the post-war British government. The process began within about six weeks of the end of the war in Europe, but was not completed until the second half of 1946. Many men and women returned from war to find that their families had died in the bombing, and that they were now homeless. And many reunited husbands and wives could not adjust to living together again after many years apart. Consequently, many marriages did not survive, often with one of the partners becoming homeless. One indicator of the social problems caused by failing marriages in the United Kingdom was the post-war divorce rate with over 60,000 applications being processed in 1947 alone.

Also, following the end of the war, Polish armed forces fighting under British command numbered approximately 195,000 and, by July 1945, this had increased to 228,000, most of the newcomers arriving in the UK having been released from prisoner-of-war and labour camps. Something like 200,000 of these Polish soldiers who had fought alongside their western allies chose not to return to a now-dominated communist Poland. So, although with some reluctance, the British government allowed them to stay in the United Kingdom. Moreover, many other East European men had fled to the UK to escape the Germans and to fight alongside the British and, like the Poles, chose not to return home. And many German and Italian prisoners-of-war also chose not to return home, some later to marry local girls.

Having obtained permission from the MOW, early in April 1946, LARDC opened negotiations with the Tyntesfield Estate Trustees and their legal representatives to allow the council to convert the site and some of the buildings into temporary housing. The parties ultimately agreed a ten-year lease commencing on 24 June 1946. For the use of the land, LARDC would pay the estate £4 per acre per year throughout the term of the lease. The trustees also agreed that all fittings, cupboards and portable wardrobes would be retained for future use, though presumably the MOW technically owned this furniture; and twenty tons of coal and coke left by the Americans after their departure would also be retained.

Sometime during the period from mid-March to mid-April, Somerset County Council also considered whether it could make use of some of the buildings. The Chief Education Officer suggested that some of the buildings might be converted into classrooms to accommodate 132 children in four classes. He also suggested that it might be possible to establish a secondary school that could ultimately accommodate 430 children.

By the beginning of April, the Ministry of Health and Somerset County Council had also become involved with the project. Representatives of the MOH and the principal housing officer of SCC visited the site to establish the suitability of the buildings for use as domestic accommodation. Their views are not recorded but, given the acute shortage of any form of new housing at that time, they were clearly not in a position to turn down LARDC's proposals.

Regardless of SCC's views, LARDC appointed an architect whose brief was to recommend how the buildings could most efficiently be converted into accommodation, and at what cost. After consultations with relevant authorities, the architect concluded that most buildings of generally robust construction on about two-thirds of the hospital site at its north-west end were suitable for conversion into housing. These included all of the original hospital ward buildings, administration buildings and miscellaneous store buildings. The buildings on the south-east side of the site used as officer's quarters, enlisted men's barracks, nurses' quarters, cookhouse and mess halls, many of timber-framed construction, were not considered sufficiently durable for conversion to permanent residences.

On 8 May 1946, the architect favourably reported his views to the LARDC meeting. He told members that, dependent upon size, each building could be converted into two-, three- or four-dwelling units at an average cost of £260 per dwelling. This figure allowed for reusing fittings and materials from other buildings that would not be retained, and included provisional sums for alterations to the electrical, water and drainage installations and supplying electric cookers. Accommodation in each dwelling would be two, three or four bedrooms, living room, bathroom, kitchen and pantry.

For simplicity, he suggested that the address of each dwelling would be the original building number plus a capital letter: A, B, C, etc. The architect further recommended that Mr Rich be appointed general foreman when building conversions got under way because of his intimate knowledge of the camp and its services.

The proposals were approved by SCC and the Ministry of Health and, later in May 1946, at the suggestion of the MOH, LARDC reopened negotiations with the trustees of the Tyntesfield Estate to allow it an option to renew the lease for a further five years after the initial ten-year lease expired. After discussions, the parties finally agreed on a three-year extension.

One of the conditions in the lease was that the site must be isolated from the remainder of the estate with an unclimbable fence, but the length fronting onto the road could be excluded from this requirement. The lease also stipulated that when any part of the site became redundant, it would be cleared, reinstated to pre-war condition and returned to estate ownership.

With the lease in place and the conversions scheme approved, LARDC invited tenders from contractors to convert wards 17, 18 and 46 each into four dwellings, and the Receiving & Information Office – building 26 – into two dwellings. In the second week of July, contracts were signed with Messrs Burston & Son and Brown & Son, and work on the first phase of conversions started towards the end of July 1946.

In late June, Somerset County Education Department decided that no buildings were suitable in which to set up a secondary school, and so the plan was dropped. It did, however, propose that the patients' mess hall and kitchen – buildings 31, 32 and 33 – and two adjacent wards would be suitable for primary school use. This proposal, however, also withered and the buildings were eventually used for other purposes. The County Medical Inspector of Health stated that he would require a building for use as a medical inspection centre and welfare clinic, not only for the residents, but also for the neighbouring district, and this facility eventually came into being.

As work on the conversions progressed, LARDC awarded further contracts early in August for converting the six surgical wards – 7 to 12 – each into four housing units. The council also decided that the covered walkway linking the operating suite to the six surgical wards would be retained and partitioned into six communal storage sheds for the joint use of the four occupiers of each ward building.

Mindful of the way in which the scheme was developing, and the numbers of people finally likely to be in residence when the scheme was completed, the Somerset County Surveyor expressed the view that an additional access at the south-east end of the camp would be desirable. But since this end of the site was not included in the scheme, the council resolved that additional access would not be provided.

By early August, the council had awarded contracts for converting buildings into thirty-four dwellings, and, a month later, in early September, such was the large number of applications for accommodation, the council decided to convert more buildings to provide another fifty dwellings.

At a council meeting on 4 September 1946, the Clerk reported that two of the units in ward building 46 would be ready for occupation within the week, and that other conversions were nearing completion and would be ready soon thereafter. The infrastructure, however, had not been improved in any way. The hardcore roads as left by the Americans were in a bad state; no proper paths to the new dwellings had been constructed; and no form of gardens had been laid down. Nonetheless, such was the desperation for somewhere to live that, during September and October, families started to move in.

Families were from all walks of life: demobbed servicemen of all ranks from officers down to privates, farm labourers, lorry drivers, school teachers, bank clerks, POWs and their new wives, Poles, Irish and many other nationalities, and those other civilians who simply had no homes to return to. One of the first families to move in was the Rew family. In 1999, Doris Christie (née Rew) gave an interview to the Nailsea and District Local History Society and this was published in PENNANT 22, the journal of the society. Extracts from that interview are reproduced here with the permission of the society and Doris. She recalls:

> I moved into Tyntesfield Park in 1946. Originally it was called Tyntesfield Estate but was re-named owing to some confusion over the house numbers of the original Tyntesfield Estate. We were among the first families to be housed, so we were not surprised to see the road up to the houses had not been surfaced (and it never was!) and the path to the front and back doors had still to be paved. But who cared? We had the house. It was pretty basic but well laid out. Two good-sized bedrooms, large living room, bathroom, kitchen and pantry. The living room was heated with a large round boiler type stove [probably an original from the hospital days], with the chimney pipe running up the room.

By the beginning of November 1946, twenty-six dwellings had been completed, and tenants were gradually moving in. At the end of the month, forty families had become tenants. Contracts had now been let for the creation of ninety dwellings and further contracts were awarded for further conversions. At the beginning of November, seventy-four workers were on site engaged on the conversion work.

Also by the end of 1946, the vicar of Wraxall organised Church of England services and Sunday school in the chapel on the site – building 3 –

and also cooperated with other religious denominations in using the chapel for non-conformist worship. Doris Christie's daughter was the first baby to be baptised there using a little silver font that Mr Warry, the local blacksmith, had made and kindly donated. The estate chapel was also used for the children's and baby clinic run by Nurse Hynam, the local district nurse.

At the end of November 1946, the original boiler house at the top of the site – building 35 – was overhauled and restarted to provide running hot water directly to occupied dwellings, supplied through lagged over-ground pipes. This was greatly appreciated by the tenants who hitherto had boiled water on their stoves whenever needed. It was not available, however, from three o'clock to half-past four in the afternoon, and from ten o'clock in the evening to six o'clock the following morning.

Lesley French took up residence after leaving the British Army late in 1947. Les recalls:

As the pipes heated up in the morning they rattled and clattered and woke people up – they didn't need alarm clocks.

In January 1947, for a three-bedroom dwelling, residents paid 9/0d rent per week exclusive of rates, water rate and hot-water supply charges, and for a two-bedroom dwelling they paid 8/0d per week. For the cold water supply, they paid 1/0d per week, and for hot water 4/6d per week. This latter charge, however, increased in mid-February to 4/9d per week. [Monetary rates are pre-decimal currency: 9/0d is now 45p, 4/9d is now approx. 24p.]

By early 1947, the site had begun to take on the character of a small village. With the population increasing, for safety reasons LARDC decided to cover the four large static water tanks still on site with netting, to the displeasure of children in the community who had quite happily swum in them. LARDC installed a telephone box, post box and a stamp vending machine near to the entrance. But although people could buy stamps and post letters, they still had to visit the post office in nearby Wraxall to collect pensions, buy postal orders and send telegrams.

The winter of 1946/7 brought with it exceptionally severe conditions. For almost the whole of December 1946, although daytime temperatures generally climbed to a little above freezing level, night-time temperatures fell below zero on twenty-eight of the thirty-one days with a minimum of −13.3°C (8°F) recorded in nearby Long Ashton on the twenty-first of the month. Little snow fell, however, and it covered the ground on only one day of the month. January saw short periods of relief from the intense cold during the first two weeks, but from the eighteenth day to the end of the month, night-time temperatures fell below zero on every night. Snow fell on eight days, blanketing the landscape for five days during the month.

February brought no respite with even worse conditions prevailing. Biting easterly winds persisted for most of the month, and although on one day the maximum daytime temperature reached 5.6°C (42°F), frost persisted throughout on eleven days. Night-time temperatures fell to or below zero on all twenty-eight days, with a minimum of –16.1°C (3°F) on the twenty-fifth of the month. Snow fell heavily on nineteen days and blanketed the ground for twenty-four days. Deep drifts formed, filling some of the narrower lanes to the tops of hedges, with numerous roads impassable for many days.

And conditions did not generally improve until the middle of March. The first two weeks of the month again brought heavy snowfalls and further deep drifts, with snow falling on nine days and lying on the ground for eight days. Daytime temperatures again hovered only a few degrees above zero, and night-time frosts persisted with a low of –17.2°C (1°F) recorded on the seventh of the month. Then, on the eighteenth, a thaw set in, and melting snow over the next week caused unprecedented flooding, but to the undoubted relief of the tenants, temperatures remained above zero for the rest of the month.

Doris Christie again:

We were living there during the very cold winter when all the country was iced up. The bus came into the estate to pick up the school children and on at least one occasion, could not turn round to go back out. People came out with buckets of ashes and sacks to put under the bus wheels, but I think eventually the buses were taken off. It was so cold that year that icicles hanging over the windows were like bars in a prison.

Local authority finances also suffered from the severe weather. At a meeting of the LARDC on 8 January 1947, the Clerk to the Council reported a general concern over the cost of providing hot water to the homes. Because of the severe weather, the growing number of tenants and the hefty fuel charge increases, the cost of providing hot water to the dwellings had risen alarmingly. But the council faced another dilemma: if they shut the boiler down at night to conserve fuel, the system might freeze up, so, by about the third week of January with the severe weather persisting, the council decided to run the hot-water boilers full-time to avoid the system freezing up, and this they maintained until the second week of March when weather conditions started to improve. The consequent increase in fuel consumption, hence cost, was considered worthwhile since a total breakdown of the system would be much more costly to put right than running the boilers around the clock.

At their meeting on 5 March 1947, LARDC again addressed the question of how best to supply hot water to the homes. By this date, ninety-seven homes had been completed and occupied, with contracts let for another twenty-two conversions. Council members deliberated about extending the piped hot-water system to those homes currently without it and to those buildings shortly to be converted. But, mindful of the huge costs incurred to date, the council decided that it would be cheaper to abandon the current method of supplying hot water and instead install electric immersion heaters and storage cylinders in all of the homes. An added benefit to the council was that the tenants would pay for the electricity to run the heaters.

However, by early June 1947, the conversions had not been implemented, and LARDC wrote to all tenants urging them not to waste hot water by leaving taps running, cautioning them that if things did not improve, periods of hot water availability would be further reduced. The letter also warned that, if tenants did not heed the advice, hot water would be available for only two days each week. But, eventually, the alternative means of producing hot water was put into service in the dwellings though the date is not recorded in council minutes.

At the end of February 1947, Somerset County Council Education Department finally decided that they would not be proceeding with plans to open any schools on the estate. Therefore, primary school children received their education at an existing school in nearby Long Ashton, and senior school children went to Nailsea secondary modern school or to grammar schools in Bristol or Weston-super-Mare.

Also at the end of February 1947, the county council expressed an interest in making use of the patients' mess hall kitchen to cook about 750 meals a day, these to be distributed to local schools in insulated containers. Certainly by early 1948, this service was operating, though when it started cannot be established for certain.

Gradually, through the spring, summer and autumn of 1947, work progressed on converting buildings constructed with brick or block walls and asbestos-cement roofs. By early September, 141 dwellings had been converted and occupied. The council's original intention was that 154 dwellings would be provided but, by this time, all of the ward buildings had been converted, and so it would be necessary to use some of the smaller ancillary buildings like the EENT clinic and the enlisted men's cookhouse – buildings 22 and 63. But the Ministry of Health were not favourably disposed to some of these buildings being used. However, a minute of LARDC's meeting held on 3 September 1947 records that '…154 dwellings have now been sanctioned and contracts let', so presumably some of the less robust buildings must have been converted and the target of 154 dwellings met. [The 1955 Electoral Role lists 156 families living in the village.]

As the number of families increased, the facilities that most large villages enjoyed at the time gradually came into being. The pharmacy – building 51 – was converted into two dwellings, one three-bedroom and the other a single bedroom, while another part of the building was fitted out as a general store. By early summer of 1947, Mr and Mrs Colley were running their thriving shop selling just about everything that the residents needed – rationing permitting. Mr Atherton, a local farmer, delivered milk daily; a greengrocer called twice a week with fresh vegetables; and Mr Holder, from Nailsea, visited fortnightly with his hardware van. A baker and butcher also made regular visits with their produce or to take orders. And another looked-forward-to visitor was the Friday evening visit by Mr Marsh and his coal-fired mobile fish and chip van. And the younger children appreciated the visits of *Bimbo*, the ice cream van. At about the same time, one of the buildings of the patients' mess hall – buildings 31 to 33 – was converted into a community hall and a social club formed, later to be followed by the opening of a cinema, and, by the autumn of 1948, the unit supply office – building 1 – had been converted into and opened as a library.

Some tenants set about improving their dwellings by building fireplaces in the lounges, and turning their plots of land into gardens and allotments in which they grew vegetables. Refrigerators were not readily available then, so enterprising Les French dug a hole in his garden and buried a large tin box in it as a cool storage for milk, etc.

'Tyntesfield village' residents on their allotments – year unknown. (Author's collection)

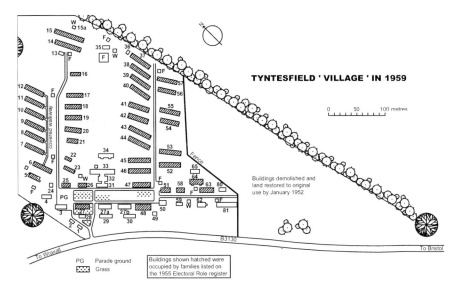

Buildings that comprised the Tyntesfield 'village' in 1959. (Author)

Another family, the Knights, took up residence in March 1948 in unit A, one of the three-bedroom conversions of the old surgical ward 10. David, one of the sons, recalls:

> *One of my first memories was the weekly visit to the estate cinema. For us children it was 6 pence a ticket to see Laurel and Hardy or Abbot and Costello followed by a main film.*

In July 1950, residents complained to LARDC about the appalling state of the ash-surfaced roads on the estate. The roads within the hospital that had served the Americans had not been improved since their departure in 1945 and were now in a bad state of repair creating quagmires in winter and dust bowls in summer. The authority promised the residents that the roads would be 're-graded to levels with stone and the whole surfaced with bituminous emulsion blended with ¼ inch stone chippings, and then rolled to falls'. Presumably, soon thereafter, these improvements were carried out since no further reference to the problem occurs in LARDC minutes.

Freda Vowles, who as a civilian had helped out in hospital ward kitchens, moved into unit C in the old ward 15. She says that soundproofing between dwellings was very poor. The ceiling followed the roof slope so, to get rid of cobwebs, she tied a brush onto the end of a number of bamboo canes, all tied together, and swished it around to knock them down.

By the early 1950s, the population of the village, conversions complete and with all dwellings occupied, had grown to around 500. So the authorities decided that the village warranted a resident policeman.

David Knights recalls:

> *A young constable with his family moved in. There were the usual couple of spivs who followed lorries waiting for things to fall off but other than that I don't think there was much crime, although at one time it did cause some embarrassment to the local headmaster when some of the hot loot of his neighbour who was the local wide boy was found hidden at the back of his shed.*
>
> *I remember a confrontation between the young constable and a bomb-happy veteran army sergeant when stopped outside his house for riding his ex-wartime motorcycle without lights soon after the official lighting up time; he was fined by the local magistrate. The constable also reported residents for other minor 'crimes' like not having a dog licence, lads playing football with a tennis ball in the road, and poaching game. The magistrate dealt with poachers severely, sometimes sentencing the unfortunates with three months in prison.*

Entertainment

Prior to December 1952 when television became available locally, the residents made their own entertainment. In the licensed social club, regular Saturday-night dances were held with visiting bands providing the music, and 'music hall' style entertainers and singers regularly performed there. Bingo was popular and the club also held a whist drive every Wednesday with people visiting from Nailsea to join in.

David Knights recalls:

> *The estate's men folk enjoyed a game of cards and snooker in the licensed social club, run by a resident steward. Teams from the Club played in the local darts, snooker and cribbage leagues and the weekly whist drive was a great attraction. The Club was also the driving force in organising the children's Christmas parties, sports days and the pantomime or the circus. One of the special treats for the younger children was the annual Chapel Sunday school coach trip to the seaside at Weymouth.*

And Les French also has fond memories of the entertainment:

> *One of the visiting singers to the club (Harry) always sang the song 'Pennies from Heaven' and people in the audience threw pennies onto the floor which were collected to provide children with a fireworks display on November 5.*

The community elders formed a youth club where, once a week, the older children could play games like table tennis and billiards, and join in gymnastic sessions, and boxing for the boys. The boys of the 'village' also formed a

Tyntesfield 'village' sports day – year unknown. (Author's collection)

Tyntesfield 'village' sports day – year unknown. (Author's collection)

Tyntesfield 'village' sports day – year unknown. Building 51 in background right. (Author's collection)

football team and sports days were regularly held. The setting for sports day was the large grassed area bounded by the upper and lower internal roads with buildings 47 and 48 at its south-east end.

In the summer months, at flower and vegetable shows, gardeners among the residents proudly showed off the produce grown in their gardens and allotments. Raffles were held and, one year in the early 1950s, Doris Christie was one of the lucky winners getting a box of groceries which, as food was in very short supply, was very welcome. Doris recalled:

> *I do not know who organised it, or who donated the prize, but it was certainly a great idea. I think we paid 6d a week towards it. [6d was pre-decimal currency; now 2½ p.]*

At Christmas time, Lady Wraxall allowed the residents to hold services in the chapel attached to the house.

Demolition of redundant buildings

In June 1947, an LARDC meeting resolved to approach the MOW to dismantle and remove the mostly timber-framed buildings on the south-east side of the site that had been deemed unsuitable for conversion into residences, reinstate the land to its former agricultural use and return it to the Estate. After lengthy discussions with LARDC the MOW decided that it had no further use for the buildings and they granted permission for the work in February 1948. But, for some reason not recorded, another three and a half years passed, and tenders inviting contractors to submit bids to carry out the work were not sent out until August 1951. LARDC in due course appointed S J Wring, a Bristol demolition specialist, to carry out the work at a cost of £1,905.

Wring started on site towards the end of November 1951 and completed their work by the end of January 1952, reseeded the soil in the spring, and so the land reverted to its former use.

Final demolition of the 'village'

Increasingly, from the middle of the 1950s, new housing estates started to rise up in nearby Nailsea, Backwell, Pill and Long Ashton, and tenants of the Tyntesfield Park village gradually moved out and into these new houses. With the lease due to expire in September 1959, at the turn of that year, Lord Wraxall started to put pressure on LARDC for repossession. In early August 1959, the council reported to Lord Wraxall that they expected that all tenants would have moved out by March 1960, and requested a further six-month extension of the lease to see this promise through. Lord Wraxall apparently agreed. In January 1960, only fifty-five tenants remained on the estate and, on 18 January, LARDC held a meeting with them to explain that the site must close by the end of March, come what may, and that the deadline was not negotiable.

Although no details are available about the tendering process for the final demolition and reinstatement of the site, LARDC records show that it let the contract to Messrs George Lawson & Son Ltd. This company ceased trading in 1968 and, sadly, twenty-five years later, all of its records were destroyed.

Despite the deadline given to the remaining tenants, the site did not become fully available to the contractor on the due date, and it is likely that demolition of some vacated buildings started while tenants who had yet to be rehoused were still living in others. Nonetheless, demolition work progressed, albeit slowly, the contractor finally clearing the site in January 1961. Ray Llewellyn recalls that a number of doors were saved and reused in some cottages dotted around the estate. And no doubt much other useful material was unofficially salvaged, to be reused in homes around the neighbourhood. Work on regrading and seeding the site with meadow grass was held over to the spring of 1961 and, shortly thereafter, LARDC returned the site to its owners.

Today

Today, almost nothing remains of the hospital or the post-war housing into which it was converted: a few square metres of concrete that formed the entrance off the Wraxall road; a few trees including two limes that stood in the island surrounded by the roads of the entrance and motor pool; and perhaps the unseen and unheard ghosts of the soldiers who died in the hospital put in occasional appearances.

Main entrance to hospital – today. (Author)

Bibliography

Alice C Boehret Collection (WV0166), Betty H Carter Women Veterans Historical Project, University of North Carolina at Greensboro

American Nursing: History and Interpretation by Mary Roberts

Bureau of Medicine and Surgery – United States Navy Medical Department at War, 1942-1945

Bureau of Medicine and Surgery – United States Navy Medical Department at War 1941-1945

'History 2nd Mobile Radio Broadcasting Company, December 1943–May 1945' written in about 1945

'History 398th Engineer Regiment by its personnel: United States of America, Scotland, England, Wales, France, Luxembourg, Belgium, and Germany, 1943-1945' written by Evert C Larson in 1945

Hospital Ships of World War II: An Illustrated Reference by Emory A Massman

Medicine under Canvas – War Journal of the 77th Evacuation Hospital

Minute Book of Bristol Health Committee – 1945/1046

Minute Book of Long Ashton Rural District Council

Operation Bolero: The Americans in Bristol and the West Country 1942-45 by Ken Wakefield published in 1994 by Crécy Books Limited

Rich Relations – The American Occupation of Britain, 1942-1945 by David Reynolds published by HarperCollins 1995

The Army Nurse Corps in World War II – The U.S. Army Center of Military History

The GIs: The Americans in Britain, 1942-1945 by Norman Longmate published by Hutchison, London, 1975

The History of Frenchay Hospital by James C Briggs

United States Army in World War II European Theater of Operations. Logistical Support of the Armies Volume I: May 1941-September 1944 by Roland G Ruppenthal

United States Army in World War II – The Technical Services. The Medical Department: Medical Service in European Theater of Operations by Graham A Cosmas & Albert E Cowdrey published by CMH Washington D.C. 1992

US Army Medical Department (AMEDD) – Office of Medical History (http://history.amedd.army.mil/books.html)

War Experiences – Benjamin Dangerfield III

Philip C Grinton, Lt Col US Army (Retired). Personal email exchanges with the author

Website: 475thmpeg.memorieshop.com

Printed by BoD¨in Norderstedt, Germany